# ASIAN-AMERICAN
# WRITERS

# MULTICULTURAL VOICES

AFRICAN-AMERICAN WRITERS

ARAB-AMERICAN AND MUSLIM WRITERS

ASIAN-AMERICAN WRITERS

HISPANIC-AMERICAN WRITERS

NATIVE AMERICAN WRITERS

MULTICULTURAL VOICES

# ASIAN-AMERICAN WRITERS

ALLISON AMEND

CHELSEA HOUSE
PUBLISHERS
An imprint of Infobase Publishing

**MULTICULTURAL VOICES: Asian-American Writers**

Copyright © 2010 by Infobase Publishing

Chelsea House
An imprint of Infobase Publishing
132 West 31st Street
New York NY 10001

**Library of Congress Cataloging-in-Publication Data**
Amend, Allison.
    Asian-American writers / Allison Amend.
        p. cm. — (Multicultural voices)
    Includes bibliographical references and index.
    ISBN 978-1-60413-313-4
    1. American literature—Asian American authors—History and criticism.    2. Asian Americans in literature.    I. Title.    II. Series.
    PS153.A84A44 2010
    810.9'895073—dc22                    2009050604

Chelsea House books are available at special discounts when purchased in bulk quantities for businesses, associations, institutions, or sales promotions. Please call our Special Sales Department in New York at (212) 967-8800 or (800) 322-8755.

You can find Chelsea House on the World Wide Web at
http://www.chelseahouse.com

Series design by Lina Farinella
Cover designed by Alicia Post
Composition by IBT Global, Troy NY
Cover printed by IBT Global, Troy NY
Book printed and bound by IBT Global, Troy NY
Date printed: April 2010
Printed in the United States of America

10 9 8 7 6 5 4 3 2 1

This book is printed on acid-free paper.

All links and Web addresses were checked and verified to be correct at the time of publication. Because of the dynamic nature of the Web, some addresses and links may have changed since publication and may no longer be valid.

# CONTENTS

# OVERVIEW

ASIAN-AMERICAN LITERATURE has existed since the first people of Asian descent began to arrive in the United States as immigrants in the 1830s. Yet as an area or topic of literary history in need of scholarly and critical attention, it was not widely known or defined until the 1970s. The rise of multicultural or ethnic literary studies, with its accompanying push to gather representative voices into anthologies, increased the exposure of many Asian-American writers. Since then, the field of Asian-American writing and criticism has expanded, but an inclusive overall definition has yet to be determined.

For the purposes of this volume, Asian-American literature consists of works written in English by U.S. residents of Asian descent. Many of these writings take place in the United States, other narratives occur in home countries, and still others in countries the authors have never visited. This volume includes a cross section of some of the most significant authors and the enduring, now canonical works they have produced. The exclusion of the wealth of literature pouring out of the pens of Asian immigrants, the absence of Filipino, Vietnamese, Cambodian, or Hawaiian writers is not a matter of aesthetic exclusion but rather of limited space. A reading list at the end of the book encourages those who are interested to explore further. The authors profiled here include women and men from China, Japan, South Korea, and India, native-born Americans and naturalized citizens.

The first Asians to establish ties to the United States came mostly as tradesmen seeking opportunity in the opening of the American West. The gold rush subsequently brought not only more Americans to California but Asians—mostly Chinese—as well, who came to seek their fortune. Railroad companies encouraged Chinese workers to settle in the West to help construct the transcontinental railroad in the 1860s. The influx was so great that many unwelcoming communities eventually passed laws barring the foreign workers from citizenship or even from taking up residence. Japanese immigrants joined the flow serving as traders and thus aiding the growth of the silk and agriculture trade. Agreements with the Philippines brought many students to the United States, and economic and educational opportunities have brought people from throughout the Asian continent ever since.

# Political History

Asian political history often forms a vivid backdrop to many of the works discussed in this volume, deeply influencing the lives and motivations of many of the characters portrayed. In general, the last 200 years have seen most of Asia's countries transition from monarchies and/or colonies to independent states. These revolutions and shifts in power occurred at different times on the continent and exacted different degrees of struggle and sacrifice. Longstanding feuds between countries and ethnic groups persist to this day, often made all the more tense and strained by difficult economic conditions. Whether a direct influence or a background element, all of these factors contribute to the poems, plays, novels, and memoirs that collectively form Asian-American literature.

## Japan

Japan's transition to a modern economy, initially occurring from the 1860s to the 1890s, was facilitated by the Meiji revolution, in which samurais overthrew the military government and created a constitutional monarchy. The new regime focused on trying to overturn the unfair trade practices the United States had forced on Japan. An attitude of welcoming Western influence led to rapid modernization and the rise of a merchant class but left some workers without jobs or a livelihood, as the island grew increasingly urban. Many Japanese moved to Hawaii to help harvest sugarcane. From there, growing numbers made the move to the American mainland.

Japanese farmers emerged as a powerful force and an increasingly visible presence on the West Coast. Immigration was stemmed by a "gentleman's agreement" in 1907, which effectively put an end to any new male immigrants (the wives of resident immigrants were granted entry, and children were allowed to join their parents). All immigration was cut off in 1924, because of labor concerns and a deepening sense of racism.

Meanwhile, imperial Japan was extending its reach and expanding its power. Through a series of wars with China, Japan gained control of Korea and Taiwan. Though hurt by the worldwide economic depression that started in 1929, Japan managed to strengthen its army, invading China in 1937 and what is now Vietnam in 1941. The United States, alarmed by Japan's increasing power, threatened to cut off trade if the Japanese did not withdraw. As relations deteriorated, World War II seemed to many an inevitable conflict. Japan bombed Hawaii in a surprise attack on December 7, 1941. The United States retaliated, eventually dropping the first atomic bombs on the cities of Hiroshima and Nagasaki in early August 1945. Overextended, its navy scattered and its army in China, Japan conceded defeat, plunging its economy into disarray and pushing many of its citizens to the brink of starvation.

Obviously, a war with Japan put many Japanese Americans in a difficult position. Americans, afraid of spies, rounded up and interned 110,000 Japanese Americans (mostly Californians) during the war, some in camps as far away as Idaho. Most were second- or third-generation Americans, as immigration had been barred starting in 1924. Japanese Americans were outraged, irate that German and Italian Americans, who also traced their origins to nations at war with the United States, were not interned as well.

Conditions in the camps were deplorable as families were separated, living conditions were unsanitary, and food was meager. Young men were offered the chance to leave the camps if they agreed to join the army. Some did so out of a sense of duty; others joined the cause in order to escape the camps and have their civil rights restored. Still others refused to fight. All male internees were forced to fill out a loyalty questionnaire. On it, questions 27 and 28 asked if they would "forswear allegiance" to Japan and fight for the United States. Those who answered *no* to each of the questions became known as "no-no boys" and were sent to jail as draft resisters.

Shunned by the Japanese Americans who fought for the United States and reviled by those Americans who hated the Japanese, these no-no boys typically came home to a hostile community that had been violated and abused by the American government. This position, in which acceptance and support were often hard to find in any community or group, is documented by John Okada in his novel *No-No Boy*.

## China

China faced its own struggles with its emergence into modernity. Throughout its long history, China was ruled by a series of emperors. A sense of isolation has long been associated with China, its Great Wall an example of attempts to keep foreign influences out.

During the 19th and 20th centuries, the humiliating loss of wars to France and Japan and the ensuing occupation of China by Japanese forces led to a prevailing atmosphere of tension in the country. Eventually, two parties came to power, the Communist Party of China and the Kuomintang Nationalist Party. When Japan surrendered in World War II, it relinquished Taiwan to Chiang Kai-shek's Nationalist Party, while the Communists gained control of mainland China. The first immigrants who arrived following the Communist rise to power, and those who escaped the Cultural Revolution (a reform movement intended to eliminate individuals and ideas perceived as threats to the Communist state), are prominently featured in or are the protagonists of Amy Tan's and Gish Jen's novels.

Once in power, Communists enjoyed a vast degree of control over the nation. Instilling Maoist doctrine, high-powered party leaders exerted influence over the citizens. Freedoms were curtailed. The press was censored. Citizens' private lives were highly controlled and often monitored. This is the background against which Chang-rae Lee, Amy Tan, and Maxine Hong Kingston's novels are set.

## Korea

Throughout its modern history, Korea has been deeply affected by the transitions, turmoil, and wars that have gripped East Asia. Japan controlled the Korean Peninsula from the second half of the 19th century until World War II, though Korean forces continuously fought to repel them. After the war ended, the country was split in half along the 38th Parallel by the United Nations. North Korea remained Communist, while South Korea emerged as a democracy. Animosity continued to build between the two newly forged countries and led to North Korea invading its southern neighbor in 1950. China and the United States became involved on their respective sides, China assisting the north, the Americans aiding the South Koreans in the conflict. The war was finally resolved by restoring the initial borders, which divide the two countries to this day. The plight of the Chinese soliders fighting in the Korean War is depicted by Ha Jin in his novel *War Trash*.

## India

India's history differs from its continental neighbors for several reasons. First, the nation is geographically cut off from the rest of Asia. India is a peninsula separated from mainland Asia by the Himalaya Mountains, which made travel difficult and dangerous. Second, India's culture developed without any significant influence from the Chinese or Japanese. Instead, India grew as a number of city-states changing hands as new empires and alliances developed. Third, its languages are Indo-European in origin rather than Asiatic.

Throughout its early history, India became an increasingly important center for agriculture and learning. The British began trading with India in the 17th century and gradually increased their presence in the subcontinent until India was annexed, made into a British colony. Treated as colonial subjects, Indians were exploited by the British Raj (or period of colonial rule lasting from 1858 to 1947), its leaders' inept policies leading to multiple famines and little benefit or economic advancement for the native Indians.

A number of resistance movements evolved, one led by the well-known nonviolent protestor Mahatma Gandhi. The British left India in 1947, and the country—the site of years of skirmishes between Sikhs, Hindus, and Muslims—was partitioned or divided into two republics: Pakistan and India. The split in the region triggered massive immigration and relocation, as people traveled to look for a new homeland, the start of a trend that has continued, in varying degrees, to this day.

# Major Influences

While each work profiled in this volume takes on its own set of conflicts and concerns, certain influences are consistently present in Asian-American literature. World War II looms large in all of these works. A catastrophic event that claimed millions of lives, the war caused hardship for years to come. The world experienced a major upsurge in immigration in the decades following the war. Modern modes of transportation and the search for economic and social freedom fueled these patterns of change. Wherever people traveled, they were sure to take at least some aspect of their homeland with them.

The religions practiced on the continent are naturally varied. Eastern Asian countries tend to consist of many Buddhist sects. Buddhism is less an organized religion than a method of inquiry into the natural world and a path to salvation. In India, religious wars and division between Sikhs, Hindus, and Muslims have marked its history for thousands of years. All these religions profess the existence of an afterlife, that the life on this planet is merely in preparation for the next one. In recent years, China's Communist state has acted much like a proxy religion, its dominating doctrines organizing the lives of the citizenry and giving them a moral code they must obey.

In India, the separation of religions gave rise to a caste system, in which the members of the highest caste rule and amass most of the wealth, while those assigned to the lowest class, the "untouchables," are extended the least amount of power and economic opportunity. Traditionally and initially, those Indians who chose to emigrate were members of the higher castes.

# Common Themes

Though the works covered in this volume are certainly diverse, many share common themes inherited from the history and culture of the region and continent that gave rise to their authors. Family is an important thread that unifies these writings, a source of conflict and pressure, identity and meaning. Whether this important influence is felt in the form of obedience to parents or in the reverence paid to ancestors, the characters typically look to their past and origins as a source of responsibility, obligation, inspiration, and pride. In each of these novels, duty and family provide a motivation and a conflict that drives the narrative forward. Obedience to parents is typically not only expected, it is an accepted fact, demanded and unquestioned.

Education also plays a major role in motivating the journeys and personal growth of many of the works' protagonists. Like people from around the world who have temporarily or permanently relocated to the United States, Asian immigrants frequently sought educational as well as economic opportunity. Education, however, does not always refer simply to acquiring knowledge or refining the intellect, and many characters acquire other forms of learning: what it means to adopt or reject the practices of another culture and the experience of being exposed to racism or labeled as an outsider.

An additional theme recurring in these books is a rich tradition of storytelling that is passed down orally throughout the generations. It is typical in many cultures to receive moral and social instruction in the form of didactic stories, tales meant to impart a life lesson as much as they are intended to entertain. Immigrants bring these narratives with them, transforming and adding to them with insights and experiences of their own.

The role of women in Asian culture is similar to the plight of many women throughout the world. Women were considered subservient to men, obedient to their fathers and then their husbands. Both Muslim and non-Muslim Eastern cultures allowed polygamy—each successive wife had less power and control over her future. Traditionally, male children were exalted; females were considered a burden. Parents usually arranged marriages, and there was little recourse for women who were in abusive relationships. This attitude and these practices, of course, have gradually changed, but the shadows cast by these systems and codes of inequality often extend far into the present. Whether in generations past or in young people making their way in the present day, arranged marriages, the horrors of physical abuse and sexual violence, and a general gender inequality loom large in many Asian-American writings. Often, the relationship between mothers and daughters is strained or distant, as attitudes and goals change and conflict.

## Conclusion

The eight authors examined in this volume all bring different and diverse cultures and experiences to their writing, yet they share common themes and concerns. From English-language writers born in other countries to those who are native Americans, the breadth or scope of literature about the Asian-American experience is vast. Individually and collectively, the authors profiled here give voice and meaning to the experiences of a large and diverse group of immigrants who have helped shape the history of the United States.

Though Asian-American writing, as a topic of study, can be characterized as a relatively new literature (as an academic subject, it has "existed" for fewer than 40 years), it is clear from the success of its authors, from the many awards and accolades they have received, and from their presence in English and literature classes and on bestseller lists, that these diverse voices have become a widely embraced and crucial part of the nation's evolving literary history.

During World War II, Japanese Americans were interned in a variety of camps located in Arkansas and throughout the American West. The experience both united and divided the individuals forced to reside in the remote detention centers and provides the background for John Okada's groundbreaking novel, *No-No Boy*.

# JOHN OKADA

## Biography

JOHN OKADA died believing that the United States did not want him. He was not exactly wrong. Born in Seattle in 1923 in the hotel his father owned, he grew up in much the same working-class circumstances as his protagonist, Ichiro, in his novel, *No-No Boy*. After war broke out, his family was interned at Minidoka, Idaho, in 1942. He was allowed to leave to enter college but then enlisted with a friend in the Air Force. He translated surrender pamphlets that were dropped over Japan and flew reconnaissance missions over Japan from his base in Guam, interpreting radio communications. When he was discharged after attaining the rank of sergeant in 1946, Okada finished college at the University of Washington, majoring in English literature. He went east for his master's degree, which he earned at Columbia University in 1949. While in New York he met his future wife, Dorothy, and after graduating, they returned to Seattle. In order to support them, he returned to school, earning a degree in library sciences.

The couple had two children, a girl and a boy, and Okada took a job at the Detroit Public Library, where he earned more money and hoped to have more time to write. The job was unrewarding, however, and Okada found employment as a technical writer. The new position left him even less time to write, and Dorothy and the children disliked Detroit (their local church did not want Japanese members), so they moved back to Seattle. Okada said of his existence at the time: "Perhaps I have been endowed with a larger capacity for normalcy than most people."

*No-No Boy* was published in 1957 and is widely considered to be one of the first novels about the Japanese-American experience. It is based on the experiences of Hajime "Jim" Akutsu, who, like Okada and his protagonist, Ichiro, was interned in Mididoka, Idaho. Akutsu, however, refused to join the army and was imprisoned for two years. The novel received little attention or acclaim when it was first released and was especially shunned by the Japanese-American community trying to reassimilate to American life.

Okada died of a heart attack in February 1971. His family was somewhat ashamed of his novel, and when they buried him in his military uniform, Dorothy did not attend the funeral. She offered his papers to the Japanese American Research Project at UCLA. They did not want them, so Dorothy burned everything, including the draft of the novel he had finished about first-generation Japanese immigrants.

## *No-No Boy*
### Summary and Analysis

The title *No-No Boy* refers to the protagonist Ichiro's refusal to fight for the United States in World War II. The book opens as Ichiro is being released from jail where he has served for two years after opposing the draft. Ichiro is an American. He was born in Seattle, where the book takes place, and lived his entire life on the same block. When his family is put in separate internment camps, he offers to fight for his country only in exchange for their reunification. Refusing this plea, the court orders him to jail. The other men at his trial have equally compelling tales. One has a brother in Japan. Though the man does not know him, he worries that he might accidentally shoot him. Another says he will fight if they give his family back his store. Still another wonders why German and Italian Americans were not subjected to the same treatment.

Ichiro experiences deep guilt at having escaped his duty to fight in the war. Most other members of his Japanese-American community fought with pride for their country. Ichiro is cursed by an old friend who spits on him for being a draft dodger. People on the street taunt him as well.

When he returns home to his store—"a hole in the wall with groceries crammed in orderly confusion on not enough shelving into not enough space"—he sees the impact of how the government treated his parents. His father barely welcomes him, speaking to his son in Japanese as his English is still rudimentary after more than thirty-five years in the United States. When Ichiro's mother arrives, she insists on putting the bread on the shelves before greeting him. Then she tells him how proud she is. "It was her way of saying that she had made him what he was."

Ichiro's mother insists that the media is lying to them, that Japan won the war. She has a letter from a friend in South America who says a boat is coming for them. Ichiro cannot comprehend his mother's willful ignorance. He tries to reason with her. "If Japan won the war, what the hell are we doing here?" But his mother refuses to believe him, and he sees how fragile her sanity is.

Ichiro's brother, Taro, age 17, comes home. Unlike Ichiro, Taro wants to enter the army. "Taro hated that thing in his elder brother." Before Ichiro can talk to him, however, he storms out of the house. So Ichiro tries to talk to his father, asking why he came to the United States. His father answers that he wanted to make money and return to Japan. Even now, after thirty-five years, he believes he will be going home soon.

Ichiro's mother makes him pay visits to the Ashidas and the Kumasakas. The Ashidas seem to share Ichiro's mother's belief that a boat will be coming soon to return them to a victorious Japan. The Kumasakas, meanwhile, have purchased a nice house, a sign that they are resigned to staying where they are. The Kumasakas treat Ichiro politely, asking if he will return to the university. When he inquires after their son Bob, he learns that Bob was killed in the war.

Ichiro returns home to find his father drinking. He joins him. His father shows him the dozens of letters from friends and family in Japan, begging for money and food or goods to sell. Ichiro asks his father why he does not show such proof of Japan's defeat to his wife. He says he has; deluded, she claims they are fakes. As he gets up to go to bed, the father says, "I'm sorry that you went to prison for us." Ichiro replies, "Sure, forget it," cutting off whatever tenuous lines of communication his father has attempted to open.

Ichiro goes to see his friend Freddie, who also served time for not agreeing to fight in the war. Freddie lives at home. He invites Ichiro to a poker game for draft dodgers, but Ichiro declines the offer; it is clear he will find no comfort in those whose experiences matched his own.

Continuing his search for a place that feels like home, Ichiro goes back to the university where he had been studying civil engineering. He sees a former professor, who assumes he did not serve in the armed forces because he had an exemption. They have a brief, generic conversation in which the professor tries halfheartedly to convince Ichiro he can resume his studies, but the conversation leaves him even more depressed than before. Searching for a connection, he receives empty platitudes instead.

Outside school, he runs into his old friend Kenji, who lost a leg in the war. The government has given him a prosthetic one, a modified car, and a scholarship to the university, but he seems as depressed as Ichiro. They drive around aimlessly, and Ken tells Ichiro how they kept amputating more and more of his leg until now only 11 inches are left. He worries that once the remaining portion begins to hurt—a sign of infection—the doctors will amputate even more, or the infection will spread and kill him.

As the friends spend the evening at various clubs, the narrator muses on the differences or contrast between the two: "They were two extremes, the Japanese who was more American than most Americans because he had crept to the brink of death for America, and the other who was neither Japanese nor American." After being teased by other patrons, Ichiro sees his brother, who asks him to come outside. Taro leads him into an alley where a group of thugs beats up Ichiro, addressing him with racial epithets and referring to him as an "it." They hit him, taunting him to say "no-no," and threaten him with a knife. Kenji appears and hits the knife-wielding man with his cane then whacks another man across the back. The attackers reluctantly leave.

Kenji drives Ichiro out into the countryside. Ichiro falls asleep, and the perspective then shifts to Kenji, who rings the doorbell of a country house. Emi, a

Japanese-American woman, opens the door. It is clear that she and Kenji are good friends. She invites him in and tells him that her husband, Ralph, still has not written from Germany after volunteering for an additional tour of duty. Her father is stuck in Japan, even though he wants to return to the United States.

Ichiro wakes up and comes in the house. Emi is struck by how much he looks like her husband. She goes upstairs. Kenji encourages Ichiro to go up with her. He climbs into her bed, and they discuss their similarities: They are both without a home, neither Japanese nor American. Ultimately, Ichiro breaks down, sobbing in her arms.

The next morning, Kenji asks Ichiro if he wants to come with him to the veteran's hospital in Portland the following day. Back home, Ichiro tells his mother he was with Kenji, and she forbids her son to see his friend again: "He is not Japanese. He fought against us. He brought shame to his father and grief to himself." Going through the mail, she places a letter from Japan in a pile "for Papa." Ichiro reads it, a plea from her sister for help; they are starving. His mother still does not believe it, however. "How they must have tortured her to get her" to reveal her secrets in order to make the letter seem authentic, Ichiro's mother says.

The narrative then shifts back to Kenji, who has gone home to visit his father and tell him that his leg is hurting. They both understand that this upcoming hospital visit is likely to be Kenji's last. His father assembles the family, where they act like any American family, watching baseball and eating dinner. Afterwards, Kenji goes out to the Club Oriental, where he thinks about the layers of discrimination in American society, the complicated relationships between blacks and immigrants, Chinese and Japanese, Jews and non-Jews. In the middle of the night, he goes to pick up Ichiro, who is happy to escape his family. While waiting, Kenji sees Ichiro's mother stacking cans in the store. When she is done, she knocks them over and stacks them again. Ichiro gets in the car and admits his mother's "snapped. Flipped. Messed up her gears."

The two friends are pulled over by a policeman in a rural town, where the local officer tries to get them to bribe him. He, too, makes fun of their heritage. Kenji refuses to play along and says he will see the cop in court. Of course, he admits to Ichiro, he fully assumes he will not live to see the court date. They pull up in front of the hospital and shake hands. Ichiro promises to come and visit Kenji. "Don't wait too long," he says.

Ichiro scours the paper, looking for a job, and finds one at an engineering company. When he gets an interview with the boss, Mr. Carrick is building a snowplow, a relatively useless item in Portland. Mr. Carrick addresses him in poor Japanese, but Ichiro is impressed that he tried. Mr. Carrick expresses his sorrow at the internment camps and offers Ichiro the job. He is kind, but Ichiro feels so guilty, taking the job from another Japanese person whom he believes "deserves it" more, that he turns the position down.

Ichiro visits Kenji in the hospital, who confirms that his leg is infected and that he will probably soon die. He tells Kenji to go back to Seattle: "Stick it through.

Let them call you names. They don't mean it. What I mean is, they don't know what they're doing. They just pick on you because they're vulnerable. They think just because they went and packed a rifle they're different but they aren't and they know it. They're still Japs."

Ichiro drives Kenji's car to Seattle. On the way into town, he stops to tell Emi that Kenji is dying. Emi cries, but Ichiro does not stay. He goes to inform Kenji's father also that his son is dying; at the news, his father seems strangely calm. He informs Ichiro that Kenji passed away earlier that afternoon, then drives Ichiro home.

Ichiro finds his father passed out, empty liquor bottles surrounding him. The bathroom door is locked. He forces it open to find his mother has taken her own life. At his mother's funeral, Ichiro is overwhelmed and near a breaking point. He leaves with Freddie, who tells him that their mutual friend Gary can get Ichiro a job at the junkyard at the Christian Center.

Back at home, Ichiro's father still at the postfuneral meal, Emi stops by to say she is sorry that she missed his mother's funeral. She says her husband asked her for a divorce and begs Ichiro to come to stay with her at her farm. He refuses but insists that they at least fulfill her desire to go out dancing. Ichiro returns to find his father packing boxes to send to Japan. He is sober, and he tells Ichiro that he does not understand what his son is going through but that he recognizes it is a major change. Ichiro has a bed, food, and spending money, his father says, and can take all the time he needs to work through his problems.

Ichiro goes to the Christian Center garage where the boss speaks some Japanese; he served in Japan for fifteen months. Ichiro admits that his situation is like Gary's—he did not serve in the army, but the boss forgives him when he expresses regret. Gary helps paint the trucks, drawing the company's logo on the side. He states that prison was a positive experience for him. He began to see clearly what he wanted. "I got the lead out . . . and the talk out of my system." Still, he sees that Ichiro is suffering. "What was unfortunate for you was the best thing that ever happened to me." Ichiro worries that he and Gary have nothing to say to each other, that they have become strangers, so he decides to turn down the job.

Freddie calls him that night and invites him out on the town. The proprietor of a pool hall is resistant to letting them in; Freddie has made trouble there before. Reluctantly, the owner agrees to let them play at the back table. Freddie gets angry and breaks a cue. When the proprietor throws them out, Freddie slings the cue ball at him. Promising he will calm down, Freddie takes Ichiro out for a "quiet drink." At the bar are friends of Eto, the man who attacked Ichiro and whom Freddie had subsequently stabbed in another fight. A scuffle ensues. Ichiro is able to hold the primary attacker off, sitting on him and punching him in the face while begging them not to fight. When the altercation seems to be over, Freddie kicks the man in the stomach. Ichiro realizes that his friend has a death wish. The man springs up and chases Freddie. Freddie gets in the car and starts to speed off but only gets across the street before the car flips and crashes, killing him. As Ichiro walks away, he thinks about all the people who have died. He resolves to rebuild his life. He embraces the glimmer of hope such a decision gives rise to, "that faint and elusive insinuation of promise as it continue[s] to take shape in mind and heart."

## Major Themes

### Personal and Cultural Identity

Identity and cultural identity are central concerns in *No-No Boy*. Ichiro struggles throughout the novel with what it means to be Japanese American. The common theme of individuals straddling two cultural worlds is explored by Okada in the novel in a new way. Ichiro is alienated from the other individuals who make up his small community. Throughout the novel, he interacts solely with Japanese and Japanese Americans. The only non-Japanese individuals he meets are the sources of insults, ridicule, and discrimination. Those with whom he is most likely to share experiences shut him out of their lives.

This schism is the origin of Ichiro's unhappiness. He is understandably bitter toward the United States, but he feels equal rancor toward those who believed themselves to be American and fought in the war while their families suffered in relocation camps.

One of the main things Ichiro and Kenji have in common is their feeling of utter hopelessness. Ichiro finally gets Kenji to admit that, even with his missing leg, he is in a better position than Ichiro is. Still, it is Kenji who literally keeps losing more and more of himself as the novel progresses. The loss of increasing portions of his leg emerges as a symbol or representation of the gradual loss of identity he experiences. Ichiro faces a similar personal atrophy or withering, one that started with his time in prison.

### Alienation

Throughout the several days in which the novel takes place, Ichiro visits every possible permutation of young Japanese American. First, the family of the war hero represents the Japanese American who declared himself wholly American and died for his beliefs. Eto, who spits on him, is the more typical Japanese American who believes that anyone who did not sign up for military service is an unpatriotic coward. There is the fellow draft dodger, Freddie, who expresses his confusion by sleeping with the woman next door and starting fights. Gary also "has the same problem" as Ichiro but is someone with whom Ichiro has nothing in common. Ichiro's brother, Taro, is embarrassed by him and joins the army to make up for Ichiro's mistakes. Taro hates his sibling to the extent that he lures Ichiro outside for a beating.

When Ichiro looks outside the community, he seems to find either understanding or discrimination, both of which feel false. His professor, though not sure who he exactly is, encourages him blandly to return to school, which makes Ichiro feel that this course of action is impossible. Then, Mr. Carrick's kindness only makes Ichiro believe that he is unworthy of the job offered him. "Ichiro knew that the job did not belong to him, but to another Japanese who was equally as American as this man." Ichiro forgives this American because he "was attempting in a small way to rectify the wrong he felt to be his own because he was a part of the country which, somehow, had erred in a moment of panic."

Ichiro's mother and father represent the extreme reactions that the older generation had to the events surrounding the war. Both are escaping the reality of their situation, that they were removed from their home and essentially held in jail for two years, and that their son was sentenced to prison for following their wishes that he not fight. Neither of his parents has learned English, and both plan to return to Japan, though it is clear that, after so many years away, there is no hope that they ever actually will. They are now alienated from much of their community because their son has chosen not to fight, seemingly proving through his actions the government's suspicion and erroneous assumption that Japanese Americans identified more as Japanese than American. Ichiro lives, while others have died, complicating matters all the more and deepening his parents' isolation from the Japanese-American community. Ichiro's mother says that Mrs. Kumasaka is no longer a part of the community because she sacrificed her son in order to prove she was American. "It is she who is dead because she did not conduct herself as a Japanese and, no longer being Japanese, she is dead."

Both parents escape the reality of their existence, the father with alcohol, the mother with fantasy. The absurd belief that Japan won the war, despite the amount of evidence to the contrary, persists, even with Emi's father, who finally realizes, after returning to Japan, the seriousness of the deprivation the people face. When Ichiro's mother is finally confronted with the truth, by her sister's letter, the despair is so great that she commits suicide. His father's reaction shows how emotionally isolated he has become, even from his own wife. He says she was mentally unstable and that it is better that she is gone, so that she no longer has to suffer.

## Disconnection and Miscommunication

Ichiro's relationship with his parents is complicated because they literally do not speak the same language. Ichiro's Japanese is rudimentary; he has trouble reading his father's letters unless they are in simplified characters. His father remembers that in the camp a lecturer unsuccessfully tried to explain the position of the younger generation and that he only managed to point out the gulf that actually existed. Ichiro blames his mother for the divide that exists between them:

> I am not your son and I am not Japanese and I am not American. . . . I do not understand you who were the half of me that is no more and because I do not understand what it was about that half that made me destroy the half of me which was American and the half which might have become the whole of me if I had said yes I will go and fight in your army because that is what I believe and want and cherish and love.

Ichiro's relationship with Emi offers another perspective or aspect of the situation. She mourns her husband, who chooses the war over his wife. She explains that it is to make up for her husband's older brother, who refused to fight. She is so lonely and disconnected that she sleeps with Ichiro because he reminds her of her husband, and the brief interlude is the one time that Ichiro feels sorrow rather than rage or guilt. "I've ruined my life and I want to know what it is that made me do it," he says to her. She understands: "It's because we're American and because we're Japanese and sometimes the two don't mix. It's all right to be German and American or Italian and American or Russian and American, but as things turned out, it wasn't all right to be Japanese and American. You had to be one or the other."

The title of the book bears examination, as it is the insult that many fling at Ichiro, "no-no boy," and the phrase that his would-be attackers try to make him say. It is an infantilizing phrase, not only in calling the adult a boy but also in making fun of a foreign speakers' rudimentary language skills, with the childish or childlike repetition of the word *no*. Another way of interpreting this key phrase is by seeing it as a double negative. The two *no*'s are another way of suggesting the affirmative, of actually saying *yes*. Saying "no no," thus, simultaneously denies and reinforces Ichiro's Japanese heritage, asserting his heritage and identity while at the same time pointing out the confusion and conflict it causes him. This is the central conflict that plagues the main character in the novel.

Still, Okada chooses to end the book on a positive note. Though Kenji, Ichiro's mother, and Freddie have died, their deaths begin to make sense to Ichiro. "A glimmer of hope—was that it? It was there, someplace." Though Ichiro will continue to struggle, Okada suggests that it is through and because of this struggle that his protagonist will find meaning.

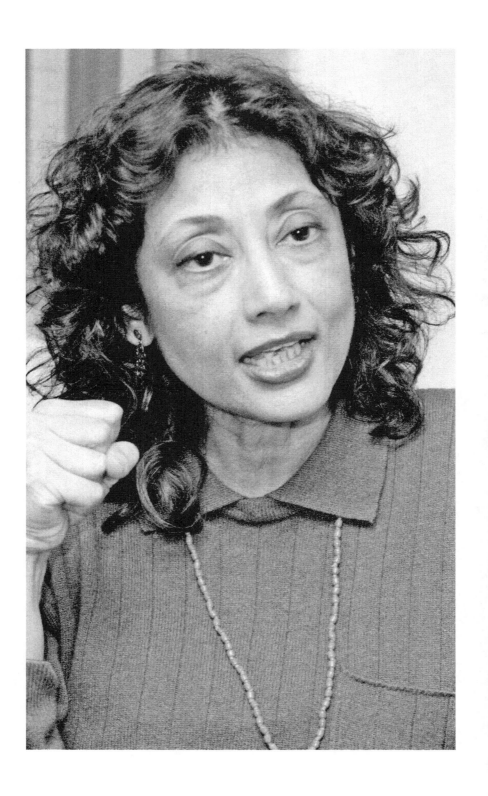

# BHARATI MUKHERJEE

## Biography

BHARATI MUKHERJEE WAS born on July 27, 1940, a little more than two weeks before India declared its independence from Great Britain. Her parents were affluent Bengalis who lived in Calcutta. An avid reader from an early age, Mukherjee knew she wanted to write since childhood and began producing stories while her family lived in Great Britain from 1948 to 1951. They returned to Calcutta where Mukherjee attended high school and college at the University of Calcutta, receiving an M.A. in English and ancient Indian culture from the University of Baroda in 1961. Mukherjee entered the University of Iowa Writers' Workshop that same year. It was there that she met Canadian writer Clark Blaise. They were married after a two-week courtship, to her parents' shock.

The couple stayed in Iowa, until Mukherjee earned her Ph.D. in English and comparative literature in 1969, and then returned to Blaise's native Canada, living for the next decade in Montreal and Toronto. They then decided to return to the United States, where Mukherjee taught at Skidmore College; Queens College, the City University of New York; and the Iowa Writers' Workshop before taking a permanent position at the University of California at Berkeley and becoming a U.S. citizen in 1989. She currently lives with Blaise in San Francisco, and the couple has two grown sons.

Mukherjee resists the label of Indian-American writer, preferring to be known simply as an American writer. In a nation of immigrants, she argues, her origins are just one more fact about her. She is known both for her short stories and novels, as well as nonfiction. *The Middleman and Other Stories* was the winner of the National Book Critics Circle Award in 1988. Additional novels include *The Tiger's Daughter* (1971), *Wife* (1975), *Jasmine* (1989), *The Holder of the World* (1993), *Leave It to Me* (1997), *Desirable Daughters* (2002), and *The Tree Bride*

(2004). In addition to *The Middleman*, she published another collection of short stories, *Darkness*, in 1985. With her husband, she has written the memoir *Days and Nights in Calcutta* (1977) and the nonfiction work *The Sorrow and the Terror: The Haunting Legacy of the Air India Tragedy* (1987). She has also written works of social analysis: *Political Culture and Leadership in India* (1991) and *Regionalism in Indian Perspective* (1992).

## *The Middleman and Other Stories*
### Summary and Analysis

*The Middleman and Other Stories* is comprised of eleven short stories that deal with migration, immigration, and assimilation. The title story is narrated by Alfie Judah, who is in an unnamed South American country, where he is the guest and employee of Clovis Ransome, a drug and gun runner. Alfie himself makes "a living from things that fall." He is escaping an investigation into a fund established to bribe judges.

Clovis invites Alfie to join him and his friend Bud as they go "deep sea fishing," code, Alfie knows, for transporting drugs, arms, and possibly medicine. He declines, interested instead in Clovis's girlfriend, Maria. The country is in the midst of a guerilla war, and it appears that the president, Guitiérrez, has allowed Clovis to reside in his country in exchange for his help.

The men leave, and Maria asks Alfie to drive her to her village. When they pull off the road, Alfie knows something is wrong. A trio of guerillas greets them, but Maria assures him they do not want him. She greets the leader, Andreas, with a kiss. (She was supposed to marry Andreas when the president claimed her as his own; he eventually traded her to Clovis who subsequently attempted to sell her to Bud.) The guerillas put Alfie in a tent, where he watches a boy torture a bird in a cage. Alfie worries they will kill him, but he and Maria get back in the now-empty truck, with the bird the boy has forced on them. Back at the compound, Clovis breaks the news that Bud was attacked and killed by guerillas; Clovis does not know how he escaped. "I suspect it helps when they're in your pay," Alfie thinks.

Clovis passes out with his hand in the birdcage, attempting to kill the animal. "Kill it," Maria begs. Alfie suggests they set it free, but Maria explains that the boy has broken its wings. "Let it out, and the crabs will kill it," she says.

Later that night, after Maria's seduction of Alfie, they are interrupted by Andreas's gang. Andreas gives Maria a pistol, and she shoots Clovis, leaving Alfie alive. Alfie accepts this as "data," just another event in his life as a middleman and one that can be turned for a profit. He concludes that in a few days he will walk to town. "Someone in the capital will be happy to know. . . . There must be something worth trading in the troubles I've seen."

"A Wife's Story" opens at a David Mamet play on Broadway in New York, where the main character, Panna, is offended by a joke about Indians, which her Hungarian companion, Imre, laughs at. They are each involved in a long-distance marriage, he to a nurse in the Hungarian countryside who is unable to get a visa to emigrate, she to a man who runs a factory in India. Panna is in the United States to pursue a master's degree. Back at home, she talks to her roommate, revealing that her marriage was arranged. Her husband calls to say that there has been an attack on one of the factory's trucks and that he is coming to visit her.

Her husband loves the United States, spending extravagantly and depending on her for practical advice. At the sightseeing tour booth, the Lebanese salesman comes on to Panna. She buys tickets for a bus tour and a visit to the Statue of Liberty. Her husband feels it is a rip-off; the island museum is closed, and they are not allowed to get out of the bus.

That evening, Panna's husband begs her to come back to India with him, but her course of studies lasts two years. She thinks about Imre. Her husband says that New York is full of cheats, and Panna feels guilty, even though he is not specifically talking about her. In the middle of the night, a phone call informs Panna's husband that there have been more attacks on the factory. Before he leaves, he wants to make love, and Panna wants "to pretend with him that nothing has changed." Later, looking at herself naked in the mirror, she imagines that she is staring at someone else.

Marshall is a Vietnam veteran and a hitman in the story he narrates, "Loose Ends." His wife, Jonda, has left him, and he is in trouble with his boss, Mr. Vee, for a contract killing that did not go as planned. Marshall found the target in question with a woman and had to kill them both.

Marshall goes to collect his money, musing about Florida, how "life goes on in Florida courtesy of middlemen who bring in things that people are willing to pay a premium to obtain." He believes that Florida is like Vietnam, corrupt and humid. He remembers visiting the London Zoo on his way to Vietnam, where he saw a python.

One night, he sees a blond swami levitate over a discount clothing store. The police arrest him, while "who knows how many killers and felons and honest nut cases watched it and politely went back to their cars?" Marshall steals a car and drives out of Miami, when he is run off the road by two men, hired goons retrieving the stolen car. They are veterans, too, and so take just the car and Marshall's cash before leaving the man on the side of a road. Marshall walks to a motel where he discovers an Indian family having dinner. Marshall refers to them as "aliens" with obvious disgust. A young woman offers to show him a room. He follows her and attacks her.

At the story's conclusion, he steals another car. "This is what I've become," he thinks. "I want to squeeze this state dry and swallow it whole," like the python.

In "Orbiting," Rindy is planning to introduce her new boyfriend to her family on Thanksgiving. Still, she cannot help thinking about her former partner, Vic, who was adored by her family. He was of Italian descent, too, and they had known each other since they were children. Now she is dating Ro, a refugee from Afghanistan.

Rindy's father brings the turkey over to defrost. He is recently retired and having trouble adjusting. Rindy then calls her sister, who is near tears after fighting with her twelve-year-old stepdaughter. Rindy tries to call Ro, but the person who answers the phone pretends not to know anyone by that name. Ro has only been in the country three months, working illegally preparing chickens at a restaurant called Little Kabul.

The family gathers, and Ro lets himself in with his key. The family members try not to display their shock. Rindy realizes that "if he asks me, I will marry him." Rindy's dad offers Ro a drink, but, a Muslim, he does not consume alcohol. Rindy's father starts humming Frank Sinatra, his own calming mantra. Ro begins to regale them with tales of his escape from Afghanistan, his torture in jail, and his long journey between airports, looking for a country that would take him in. He describes his job as a chicken gutter in detail, showing his ritual dagger.

Rindy's father sharpens the carving knife, but Rindy puts the turkey down in front of Ro. He takes his dagger and carves the meat perfectly. Rindy feels a rush of love. "I shall teach him how to walk like an American, how to dress . . . how to fill up a room. . . . Ro is Clint Eastwood, scarred hero and survivor. Dad and Brent [her brother-in-law] are children." She believes that Ro can be remade, a better American because of his foreign birth than those born here can ever hope to be.

Griffin, the stock broker narrator in "Fighting for the Rebound," claims to love his girlfriend, Blanquita, a Filipino immigrant living in Atlanta. In Manila, she grew up in a house of servants and luxury, but in the United States, her father stocks liquor store shelves, her mother runs a hair salon in her kitchen, and Blanquita is a makeup artist. She starts a fight, claiming that Griffin is a "racist, patronizing jerk," if he thinks she is beautiful instead of simply different from his previous girlfriends. "There's a difference between exotic and foreign, isn't there?" Griffin wonders. He peers around her, trying to watch wrestling on television.

Blanquita announces that she is going away for the weekend with a man named Chief, but Griff does not succumb to the attempt to make him jealous. Throughout, he compares Blanquita to his other girlfriends, using financial metaphors. For Blanquita, the fight dredges up memories: "Love flees, but we're stuck with love's debris." Alternating between feeling needy and aggressive toward Griff, she goes away with Chief.

Lonely, Griff goes to the mall where he picks up "a Buckhead version of Liv Ullmann" in a frame shop. They make love and speak about being "a good team." Then the phone rings. It is Blanquita, begging Griff to come get her. He leaves the woman in bed and heads off to go pick up Blanquita.

Maya Sanyal is not the ideal woman that everyone imagines she is in "The Tenant." She is divorced; she has slept with many men, none of whom is Indian. She has recently moved to Cedar Falls, Iowa, to teach comparative literature. Doing what she has always done in a new American town, she looks in the phone book for other Bengali names to attempt to gather the spices essential to the dishes she prepares. A colleague asks her if Rab Chatterji from the physics department has called.

Outside her apartment, her landlord, Ted Suminski, watches her leeringily as he plays darts. Dr. Chatterji calls, using his official title. "An old-fashioned Indian, she assumes." He invites her to Sunday tea. Maya is unsure if she is imagining it, but she thinks she sees her landlord throw a dart toward her window.

Dr. Chatterji seems pleasant when he picks her up, and she asks him to call her Maya when he calls her Mrs. Sanyal. His wife is plump and friendly, inviting her in for a feast of traditional food. There are several noises coming from upstairs, which everyone ignores. Mrs. Chatterji wants to hear about Maya's famous family, which is involved in various political scandals. Finally, it is revealed that the noise upstairs is Mrs. Chatterji's nephew, come to the United States to study. Suddenly, to Maya, the Chatterjis look old and tired, vain. They are upset because the nephew is in love with a "Negro Muslim," a match their Brahmin caste cannot support.

Mrs. Chatterji plays the harmonium, singing a traditional hymn. Despite herself, Maya is moved by the woman, who is obviously devoted to her religion. When Dr. Chatterji drops her off, he comes on to her. All Maya can say is, "Dr. Chatterji—really!"

The next day, Maya looks at the Indian newspapers advertising relationships. She calls Ashoke Mehta who has a pleasing voice. Maya thinks, "Yes, you who are at ease in both worlds, you are the one." She arranges to meet him in the airport and feels he is the "man of [her] dreams." They speak only briefly but feel an immediate connection.

When Maya returns home, her landlord asks her to move out; he is getting remarried and wants to live in the apartment. Two months later, she finds a new apartment and begins to date her new landlord, a man named Fred who has no arms. "Two wounded people," he calls them. "It will shock her, this assumed equivalence with a man so strikingly deficient. She knows she is strange, and lonely, but being Indian is not the same, she would have thought, as being a freak."

A few months later, the phone rings. It is Ashoke Mehta. He says he had to take care of a problem. He hears Fred's voice in the background, but insists just the same that she come live with him. Maya thinks, "When she moves out . . . it will not be the end of Fred's world."

In "Fathering," Jason is a divorced Vietnam veteran, raising, with his girlfriend, Sharon, his recently discovered half-Vietnamese child. Eng bursts into their bedroom, saying she is hungry. Sharon, fed up, is curt with the child, but Jason thinks she is ill. Eng is fascinated by Jason's scars. She shows him scars and marks of her own, little circles of brown and blue bruises.

Sharon calls the doctor, believing that Eng needs psychiatric help, but Jason continues to think that she has the flu. Sharon goes out for aspirin. Upstairs, Eng has a nightmare that someone is trying to shoot her grandmother. It is a violent dream, and she lashes out.

The doctor calls. Sharon has arrived at his office hysterical. They gave her a sedative, so she will need to be picked up. In the car, Eng asks for a quarter. Jason gives her one and she responds, "Thanks, soldier," still speaking the English she learned as a child living on the streets in Vietnam.

Back at home, Sharon rests on the sofa. "If you love me, send her back," she says. Behind him, Eng choruses: "She's bad, Dad. Send her back." The doctor examines Eng, who bites him. "Don't let him touch me, grandma!" Eng screams, obviously hallucinating. She takes off all her clothes and begins to shout, taking the quarter and turning it in circles on her arm until round bruises form to match the other ones. Her speech becomes less intelligible: "Get the hell out, you bastard! Bang bang! . . . Scram, Yankee bastard!"

Jason panics. "Something incurable is happening to my women." He then decides what course of action he will take. "Coming pardner," he whispers to Eng. "I jerk her away from my enemies. My Saigon kid and me: we're a team." Father and daughter leave together.

Jasmine is a Trinidadian of Indian descent in the short story "Jasmine," which will loosely form the basis for Mukherjee's novel of the same name. Jasmine arrives in Detroit after being smuggled across the border. She works as a maid in a hotel run by Trinidadian Indians, a job she hates. One weekend, she travels to Ann Arbor to attend concerts. "She knew Ann Arbor was a special place." So she spends the night at the university's student union and goes to the placement office the next morning.

Jasmine finds work as a nanny for Bill and Lara Moffitt. Bill is a professor, Lara a performance artist. Their daughter, Muffie, is nearly self-sufficient. Bill and Lara treat Jasmine like family, and she considers herself lucky. Her assimilation into American life is made all the more obvious when she returns to the motel for the holidays and the owners treat her as "whitefolk-fancy."

Lara and her performance troupe go on a long road trip. One night, Bill invites Jasmine to dance. He holds her close and begs her to have sex with him. "Come on, baby," he says. "You're really something, flower of Trinidad." "Flower of Ann Arbor," she replies, as she concedes to his wishes, making her transition to American complete.

In "Danny's Girls," Danny Sahib is a man of local importance. He has been on his own since the age of six, running local scams, scalping tickets, and ultimately importing mail-order brides. The narrator works for him. He is an Indian whose parents were deported from their home in Uganda. His father ran off soon after they arrived in the United States. The narrator lives with his aunt, who runs a boarding house for women waiting to find American husbands.

The narrator falls in love with a Nepalese woman who takes the name Rosie. She is exciting to the narrator, speaking in a polished British accent: "Smashing. . . . Jolly good." The narrator contemplates the strange divide between the supposedly respectable woman he is expected to marry and the kind of woman, like Rosie, who he thinks would actually make him happy. Rosie thinks she can get a green card, become a legal resident, without getting married. Danny makes fun of the narrator, calling him a eunuch (or castrated male). Suddenly the narrator realizes that by handing out flyers with available women's pictures on them, by creating publicity for Danny's marriage brokerage, he is effectively offering the women as commodities. Angry, he grabs an umbrella and storms up to Rosie's room, smashing it on the bed. Rosie calmly says, "So, you want me, do you?" She brings him into her bed, the narrator observing, "for the first time I felt my life was going to be A-Okay."

In "Buried Lives," Mr. Venkatesan is a middle-aged literature teacher who finds himself embroiled in the conflict in Sri Lanka. He is not a political man, but he has raised his young sisters, one of whom has taken up with a Tamil Tiger, a member of the guerilla resistance force. Marching in a protest, the young woman gets up on a car. A group of Buddhist policemen attempt to force her down, pulling her hair and hitting her. Mr. Venkatesan swings the axe he is holding, and it injures a policeman. Mr. Venkatesan runs away, fleeing to his school, where he begins his lesson on the poet Matthew Arnold. Embarrassed by his emotion, he yells at the one student who reveals that he, too, has a passion for poetry.

Mr. Venkatesan decides to look into emigrating, but there is no legal option. A fellow teacher says she is leaving, having secured work as a domestic. Mr. Venkatesan makes fun of her decision, applying instead for a scholarship to eight American universities, all of which reject him.

His sister's guerilla boyfriend is involved in a prison break and must flee to the countryside. Reluctantly, Mr. Venkatesan gives his blessing for his sister to join him. The boyfriend says he will put Mr. Venkatesan in touch with someone who can help him emigrate.

The agent books him a complicated passage to Canada via Hamburg, Germany. He begins his journey, with his fake travel papers, by taking a boat to the island of Tuticorin, the same islands "Mr. Venkatesan's ancestors had left to find their fortunes." On Tuticorin, he is greeted by the Tamil Tigers as a hero who threw an axe at a demonstration. He takes a train to Madras, another to Delhi, and then flies to Tashkent and then to Moscow. From there, he travels to Berlin, sneaking across the still-closed border to Hamburg. Though he has paid to get to Canada, his connections strand him in Hamburg, where a man named Rammi offers his services, bringing Mr. Venkatesan to a hotel and agreeing to help him find passage. Rammi's cousin is a beautiful widow named Queenie, who runs the hotel with help from her daughter. Mr. Venkatesan falls immediately in love with the older woman.

A legitimate tourist comes to stay at the hotel and is given the one good room. Mr. Venkatesan is assigned a bunk bed in a room with other illegal immigrants. He knows without being told that he should stay out of the German guest's sight. He also notices that Queenie's daughter has been stealing from the men.

When Queenie comes to tell him that Rammi is close to arranging his passage, Mr. Venkatesan blurts out, "I love you." He follows Queenie to the kitchen where her daughter shows him her cache of stolen items. Suddenly the German hotel guest appears, angry at being robbed. He yells at them in English. "You filthy swine. We don't want you making filthy our Germany."

Mr. Venkatesan is terrified the man is going to report him. The German tourist picks up the pay phone and calls the police. Mr. Venkatesan imagines a future in jail, but suddenly Queenie blurts out, "You're harassing my fiancé. He's a future German citizen. He will become my husband."

In "The Management of Grief," Shaila Bhave is mourning the loss of her husband and two sons in an airplane accident, which she is sure was caused by a Sikh bomb. The entire Indian community in Toronto is affected, as most had relatives and friends on the airplane. Each has a different reaction to the tragedy.

Kusum, Shaila's neighbor, lost her younger daughter, her favorite, who sang beautifully. The older one, Pam, stayed behind because she had a job she liked at McDonald's. "You think I don't know what Mummy's thinking?" she accuses. "Mummy wishes my little sister were alive and I were dead." It is a horrible accusation but one that has the ring of truth to it.

Shaila receives a visit from Judith Templeton, a government appointee, who needs her to help bridge the cultural divide between the government agencies and the Indian families. Shaila considers herself a freak because of the eerie calm she cannot seem to shake, despite her recent loss. She worries that she never told her husband she loved him.

Shaila travels to Ireland where bodies are being pulled from the ocean. Kusum talks about fate, while Shaila relies on valium. Shaila thinks about her sons' strong swimming ability. Dr. Ranganathan, an electrical engineer, tells her that the ocean is dotted with archipelagos and helps her believe it is possible that her sons swam to safety after the crash.

The Irish throw roses into the sea to commemorate the dead, after the newspaper reveals it to be an Indian custom. They approach the mourners, who are obvious because of their skin color and appearance, and hug them.

Officials bring Shaila in to look at photographs. The images bear a resemblance to her sons, but the faces are wider, distorted. The officials try to tell her that the water makes the bodies puffy, that the bones in their faces have broken. Still, Shaila says they are not her sons, that she does not mean to be crying. She is happy to cling to the hope that her sons are still alive.

Shaila travels to India, where "I become, once again, an only child of rich, ailing parents." Friends come to pay their respects, but Shaila cringes when she sees Sikhs, who are blamed for the bomb that brought down the plane. The families of the survivors encourage the men who lost their spouses in the crash to remarry, but the recently widowed women are not afforded the same freedom. Shaila's family wants her to stay in India, but she wants to return. "I am trapped between two modes of knowledge. . . . Like my husband's spirit, I flutter between worlds.

One day, while making an offering at a temple, Shaila sees her husband's spirit. "You must finish alone what we started together," he says. Shaila knows she must return to Canada. Kusum puts her house up for sale and goes to live in an ashram, a secluded religious community, in Hardwar. Dr. Ranganathan calls Shaila often. He cannot bring himself to sell his house, even though he now works more than a hundred miles away. Shaila continues to see and hear her husband and sons at night.

Judith Templeton asks Shaila to help her get through to a Sikh couple who cannot receive their son's death benefits until they sign legal documents. Shaila does not admit to Judith that she is now mistrustful of Sikhs. When Shaila tries to tell them that their electricity and water will be cut off, they claim that God will provide. They believe that their sons will return. To sign documents is to admit that they are gone.

Kusum writes from her ashram to say that she is able to communicate with her dead husband and daughter; Shaila is envious. She no longer has visions. Then, suddenly, she hears a voice: "Your time has come. . . . Go, be brave." So, without knowing where she is walking, she begins her journey, leaving behind the pain of her recent past.

## Major Themes

### The Diverse Immigrant Experience

A collection of stories is held together by its ability to present and maintain consistent themes through its various plots and characters. Though Mukherjee's novel *Jasmine* deals more specifically with the Indian immigrant experience, *The Middleman and Other Stories* takes as its central topic the notion of American immigration in general. Stories such as "Fighting for the Rebound" and "Orbiting" look at immigration from the point of view of someone in a relationship with the immigrant. Other stories, including "A Wife's Story" and "The Tenant," are told by the immigrant himself or herself. There are also stories focusing on individuals who are immigrants in their own country—"Loose Ends"—and those whose travels take them to countries other than the United States, such as the collection's title story.

Because of the multiple points of view the various stories contain, the collection takes on a significance greater than merely that of one culture's experience. The book instead reflects the stories of everyone who feels that they live between worlds. A Vietnam veteran who feels that Florida is an alien landscape, or a father who identifies with the terror and victimization of his half-Vietnamese child, is as much an immigrant or an outsider to American culture as an exchange student.

### Racism and Stereotype

Another common thread uniting the stories is the racist attitudes of many Americans. Minorities are called a variety of racial slurs and epithets by people born in the United States, even by the characters' fellow immigrants. The last story in the collection explores how people of the same culture but of different religions can be led to hating one another through an act of violence.

Similarly, Mukherjee examines the stereotypes that surround Indian immigrants and immigrants in general. Characters find Indian families running hotels, eating spicy food, and wearing traditional clothing. Some immigrants come to the United States to study but live as though they were still in their home villages. By giving these characters voices and stories, Mukherjee humanizes these common images and allows the reader insight into the psyches of her characters.

Many of the women in these stories suffer from not only male aggression and control but also society's overexoticized image of themselves. They are objects of desire because they are different, or exotic, not because of who they, in essence, are. In "The Tenant," Maya is seen as so divorced from her native culture she is compared to a man without arms. When Bill calls Jasmine the "flower of Trinidad," he brings attention to her foreignness, her status as the "other," even though she corrects him by identifiying herself as the "flower of Ann Arbor." She is interested in education and assimilation; he finds her attractive only in the context of being a foreigner.

## Tradition, Assimilation, and Change

The desire to establish an independent identity, free of racism or cultural stereotype, in turn leads to a struggle between the "old ways" and the "new ways." In its most obvious form, this is manifest in how the characters address one another. Traditional Indian women do not call their husbands by their first names. Mukherjee explores this theme through clothing and dress as well. By giving up saris to dress in a more Western manner, Indian women acquire "reputations" within their own communities, seen as too aggressively or actively embracing American ideals and standards of beauty and appearance. The idea that a woman can chose her own partner is radical, and the struggle to balance expectations at home in India with newfound freedom and diverse customs and cultures places undue stress on the characters.

Mukherjee's characters are not always good people. They are criminals and adulterers; they take advantage of those less fortunate. Nonetheless, they are portrayed as frank, and Mukherjee gives her readers an unflinching portrait of their lives. Her ability to mimic immigrant speech patterns is impressive. She is able to realistically assume a variety of first-person voices (only two of the stories are told in the third person) and convincingly present those personas. The vivid realism she brings to her characters gives Mukherjee license to explore all sides of the immigrant issue, giving the reader a glimpse of the lives of those individuals the Untited States has granted entrance to but not always welcomed.

# MAXINE HONG KINGSTON

## Biography

IT SOUNDS LIKE the setup for a bad joke: Maxine Hong Kingston and Alice Walker are sharing a jail cell. . . . Yet this scenario occurred on March 8, 2003, when Kingston and Walker were arrested while protesting the war in Iraq. This is just another episode in the life of writer, provocateur, activist, and feminist Maxine Hong Kingston.

Born on October 27, 1940, in Stockton, California, Kingston was the first child of her family to be born in the United States (two older siblings were born in China.) In China, her Cantonese parents were a midwife and a scholar; in the United States, they ran a gambling parlor and a laundry, the center of their Chinese-American community. Her childhood was marked by stories told by her relatives. Kingston was a precocious writer; she won $5 in an elementary school contest and continued to write throughout her early years.

Despite her talent for the written word, she majored in engineering at the University of California at Berkeley, where she met her husband, actor Earll Kingston, in an English class and switched her major to her real love, literature. They married in 1962, and Kingston's son was born the following year.

Worried about supporting her family, Kingston went back to Berkeley to earn a teaching certificate and taught high school math and English. In 1967, the Kingstons grew increasingly concerned about their future. The antiwar movement they had been participating in was getting increasingly violent, fueled also by prevalent drug use. The Kingstons sought a more tranquil place to raise their family and ended up in Hawaii.

Kingston's first book, *The Woman Warrior: Memoirs of a Girlhood among Ghosts*, was published in 1976 to tremendous acclaim. It received the National Book Critics Circle Award the same year. At the ceremony, Kingston, who is only 4 feet 9 inches tall, had to bend around the podium to give her acceptance speech. The book's success allowed Kingston to write full time; she published *China Men* in 1980, which won the National Book Award for general nonfiction. In 1990, the Kingstons returned to Berkeley, where she has taught creative writing ever since.

*Tripmaster Monkey: His Fake Book*, her first novel, was published in 1989. Based on her own experiences in the 1960s, the novel is widely taught because of its unusual style and subject matter. Her first trip to China occurred in 1984, even though she had been writing about the country all her life. Other books include *Hawaii One Summer* (1987), *Through the Black Curtain* (1987), *To Be the Poet* (2002), and the anthology *Veterans of War, Veterans of Peace*. In 1991, the novel she had been working on, *The Fourth Book of Peace,* was destroyed in a fire in her home. She began it again as the *Fifth Book of Peace*; it was published in 2003. Though Kingston has won many awards and received many distinctions—including a National Endowment for the Arts grant, the American Book Award, and the PEN West Award—her highest honor was bestowed on her by President Bill Clinton in 1997. At the White House, she accepted the National Humanities Medal, the nation's highest artistic honor.

Kingston has been hailed as the godmother of Asian-American fiction, paving the way for subsequent authors such as Amy Tan and Gish Jen. Her books weave myth, memoir, and fantasy into narratives that capture what she considers to be her own experience, not necessarily representative of all Chinese-American experience. She has been criticized by other Asian-American authors for watering down and altering Chinese myths, willfully misinterpreting them to make them palatable for a non-Chinese audience. She counters that argument by asserting that she is continuing the tradition of storytelling, which necessarily includes revision and adaptation of the tales. She also says that by the mere act of writing about the Chinese-American experience, she is carving space for herself in her homeland, "claiming America" as her own.

## *The Woman Warrior: Memoirs of a Girlhood among Ghosts*
### Summary and Analysis

*The Woman Warrior: Memoirs of a Girlhood among Ghosts* is Maxine Hong Kingston's first book. It is an autobiography/memoir published as a companion volume to the later work *China Men*. In it, Kingston recounts her childhood and family history using memory, storytelling, myth, and fantasy. Therefore, while it is not a strict retelling of her life, it nevertheless is a personalized account of its formative events. The narrator, then, is referred to as Kingston, even if at times the book becomes more like a novel than a strictly fact-based memoir.

The book opens with the chapter "No Name Woman." Kingston's mother, Brave Orchid, tells a teenaged Kingston the story of the aunt she never knew about. In rural China in 1924, several men from Brave Orchid's village leave for the United States. In order to maintain ties to China, they marry local women before they go. Years later, in China, Brave Orchid's sister-in-law becomes pregnant. The villagers shun her, raiding the house the night the baby is due. She gives birth, alone in a pigsty, to a baby girl, before drowning herself and the child in the well.

Kingston considers the possible scenarios for the aunt's actions. She may have met a lover, but more likely she was raped. She wonders, too, how true the story is. Brave Orchid tells the story as if she were there at the house the night it was raided, which is impossible, since according to Chinese custom, a wife lives with her in-laws and the two women would not have shared a home. Because she committed suicide, the aunt is never mentioned by anyone in the family, including Kingston's father.

The aunt killed herself during a difficult time in Chinese history. There was, according to Kingston, a drought, a plague of ghosts, and a continuing war with the Japanese. The aunt's misbehavior would have cursed the village. The raid on the house was intended to rid the community of the curse. Again, Kingston recounts the story of the child's birth, this time imaging that the aunt nursed her before she took the newborn to the well. To spare the child a life of hardship, perhaps the drowning was an act of love more than an act of desperation.

Brave Orchid tells Kingston that she must never mention the aunt again. Kingston understands that by pretending the aunt never existed, she is participating in the punishment. Still, for twenty years she keeps her mother's confidence. All that time, according to Chinese lore, her aunt's ghost would have been unhappily fighting for sustenance. A departed soul must be remembered for it to find peace.

In the next section, "White Tigers," Kingston examines the legend of the female warrior. She imagines a seven-year-old girl who, lost in the mountains, finds a hut inhabited by two elderly gurus. The girl spends the night. The following morning the couple asks if she would like to stay with them and train to be a warrior. In a gourd of water, the girl can see her parents. They understand she has been called to a higher purpose and do not object. She studies martial arts, magic, and strength and undergoes an initiation rite attended by visions of white tigers and dancing figures moving through time. Their attire keeps changing according to their advancing ages.

The girl also begins dragon training. On New Year's Day, she is allowed to view her parents in the water gourd. In it, she also sees that in her other life she is marrying a childhood friend, which pleases her. When her training is finally complete, she makes a sword appear from the sky and is given fifteen white beads in case of danger. She then returns home, where her parents carve all their grievances into the skin on her back, so she will know how to seek revenge. Men join her assembling army and they head north, slaying a giant and the emperor's troops along the way. She never tells her army that she is a woman—lying about your gender is a crime in Chinese society. Her forces finally meet up with the emperor, behead him, and select a peasant to rule in his place. Heading home, she confronts the baron who has had a viselike grip on her family. He mocks her for being a woman, and she exposes the carvings on her back, before beheading him. The woman warrior then settles down to help her family and produce sons.

Here, the narrative shifts from the fantastical nature of Kingston's dream about the woman warrior to the parallels these tales have in her own life. She describes how she has always felt like a disappointment. Her good grades and eventual admission to the prestigious University of California at Berkeley do not measure up to the warrior's feats that her mother describes. She is not sure where exactly her personal village, or her place within American society, is. She also associates traditional female tasks with slavery, so she refuses to cook or clean. Kingston believes that her feet are bound by her Chinese heritage.

Kingston continues describing her personal wars. She objects to her paint-store boss's characterization of a color as "nigger yellow." She is fired from her job when she refuses to work to support a restaurant that is picketed by the National Association for the Advancement of Colored People and the Congress for Racial Equality. She opposes the Communists who have China under such tight control, taking land and punishing the family members that remain. Closer to home, she wants to avenge her family by reclaiming their laundry businesses in New York and California.

News from Communist-ruled China is confusing—family members have disappeared, businesses have been seized, people have been relocated. Her parents feel guilty for not sending money. Kingston compares her family to the warrior's family. They are lucky to be living in the United States and have less to avenge than the warrior does. Trying to find her place in the world, Kingston moves to Hawaii and lives among other Asian Americans, but they are not her "village," she concludes.

In "Shaman," a young Kingston opens a tin to find the room flooded with the smell of China. Brave Orchid's medical diploma rests inside. Kingston compares the solemn faces of her parents in China to their smiling poses in the United States, especially her father. Kingston discovers that her mother is actually 10 years older than she admits to being and had two children who died as toddlers. While in China, both her children die as toddlers. When her mother decides to be a doctor, she is assigned to a room with five roommates and is excited to have a space of her own for the first time.

Brave Orchid is an excellent student, allowing others to copy her exam papers. She studies harder than she lets on, since she is almost twenty years older than most of the students. The other students are afraid of a haunted room at the school, and they ask Brave Orchid to look into it. Bringing a knife and a novel, Brave Orchid is courageous enough to spend the night in the room. If the students find her unconscious, she instructs, they should tweak her earlobes and call her name until she comes to.

Scared, Brave Orchid reads out loud. A furry Sitting Ghost rushes out from under the bed, pinning Brave Orchid down. She struggles, insulting and fighting the apparition, threatening to burn it out of existence. Finally the ghost leaves, and Brave Orchid sleeps. When the students come to get her the following morning, she mysteriously says she died at three a.m. for twelve years. She describes a ringing noise, and the young women burn incense to smoke out the ghost. They find a bloody piece of wood under the bed. Burning it releases a smell like singed human flesh.

Kingston admires the women in the medical school as pioneers changing the mores of Chinese society. Brave Orchid's friends become her family, the relatives whose names soothe her. Kingston wonders if the change in these rituals causes her mother's delay in finding her way. When she finishes medical school, Brave Orchid returns to her village, wealthy and respected. She buys a slave girl, to train as a nurse, at the market, who Kingston suspects Brave Orchid loves more than her own children. She says she paid $50 for the slave; it cost her $200 to have Kingston.

Brave Orchid frightens Kingston with tales of the babies she delivers, those with blue eyes obtained from ghosts and another who had no anus and was left to die. She describes how newborn girls were smothered in ashes. She says that she was chased by ghosts and once a half-man, half-ape creature. Kingston says she often dreams that she is taking care of babies, as her mother does, but ends up hurting them. She is glad to realize it is only a dream. She traces the source of her nightmares to her mother's tales. "Before we can leave our parents, they stuff our heads like the suitcases which they jam-pack with homemade underwear."

In 1940, Brave Orchid makes the journey to the United States where she is no longer a doctor; instead she is a midwife. For her, the new country is as full of ghosts as China is. Taxi drivers, policemen, newsboys and garbagemen are all ghosts, trying to lure children to the gypsies, who will boil them into ointment. Kingston's childhood is filled with fear and superstition. Kingston is afraid of going to China, worried that her parents will sell her as a slave and that her father will take additional wives.

Brave Orchid says that in the United States people spend their lives working, while in China people understand how to slow down and appreciate one another. Kingston replies that time is the same all over the world. Their talk turns to new Chinese immigrants, fugitives from Communism. Brave Orchid says she wants all her children to return home, an idea that gives Kingston a "spider headache," making her feel burdened by or responsible for the entire world. She explains that when she is not around Brave Orchid she does not get sick, and that her life is best lived without ghosts. Her mother calls her "Little Dog," so that the gods do not think she loves her too much.

"At the Western Place" is the book's fourth section. Brave Orchid waits at San Francisco Airport for her sister, Moon Orchid, to arrive from Hong Kong. She has not seen her sister in years and has only now managed to get her a visa—and then only by arranging a marriage for Moon Orchid's daughter to a Chinese-American man. When Moon Orchid steps off the plane, neither sister recognizes the other; they have both gotten old.

Brave Orchid appears to be confused. She does not believe that her son is stationed in the Philippines and seems convinced that the army has sent him to Vietnam. It is a confusion she shares with her sister, who does not adjust well to life in the United States. Moon Orchid's husband has always sent her money, but he has moved on with his life and has a new family in Los Angeles. Brave Orchid thinks her sister should be angry and demand her place as first wife back; but Moon Orchid is unsure. She is timid and afraid of jeopardizing her husband's support; he was the one who paid for their daughter to go to college. Moon Orchid's daughter wants to look for her father, too, even though he has never responded to her letters saying that she also lives in Los Angeles. Reluctantly, Moon Orchid agrees.

Each Orchid sister feels sorry for the other. Moon Orchid's husband is cruel, while Moon Orchid thinks that Brave Orchid's children are silly and rude. They smell like milk, she says, and stare at her and only respond to compliments. Similarly, Moon Orchid does not approve of the family pictures on the wall, even though her sister says they are permitted in the United States.

Brave Orchid's son then drives them to Los Angeles and finds the office building where Moon Orchid's husband works. He is a doctor, and his new wife is the receptionist. The son tells him that someone broke her leg outside, and the doctor comes down. He does not recognize the women and calls them "grandmother." When they reveal who they are, the husband says that he is a different person now. China was like an old book; Moon Orchid was just a character in it. He will continue to support her, but he does not want her in his life.

Moon Orchid lives with her daughter in Los Angeles, but she withdraws more and more from life. Finally, Brave Orchid calls, but Moon Orchid hangs up on her, believing that Mexicans who live in the area are terrorizing her and listening in on her phone calls. She moves away but remains irrationally scared of Mexicans. It is obvious her sanity is waning. Brave Orchid sends for Moon Orchid, who steps off the bus looking deathly thin. Her condition deteriorates, and she is finally sent to a mental-health facility.

Brave Orchid is surprised to find her sister happy there. No one leaves, she says, and she is surrounded by her daughters. Moon Orchid dies in her sleep, and Brave Orchid decides that this is an omen that she will die soon too. She begs her children not to let their father remarry; she tells her daughters they should never allow their husbands to be unfaithful.

In "Song for a Barbarian Reed Pipe," Kingston examines the source of her storytelling nature. Her mother cut Kingston's frenulum when she was a child so that she would not be tongue-tied. Perhaps, she believes, that is the source of her childhood silence. She never spoke and struggled in school.

Instances of cultural misunderstanding abound in their lives. Kingston recalls a time when a pharmacy misdelivered an order. Brave Orchid took the children to the store and demanded candy as a reparation. The pharmacy employees think that the family is begging, expecting handouts, while Brave Orchid believes she is teaching her children manners.

There are other cultural differences. Chinese music sounds strident to American ears, and Americans are shocked at Chinese behavior at concerts. Kingston is referred to speech therapy, where she is able to speak normally for the therapist, speaking in a whisper she describes as American feminine. She worries that silence is akin to insanity.

Another silent girl attends school with Kingston, who hates the quiet student, recognizing what she dislikes in herself. In the bathroom alone one day, Kingston begins to tease the girl, pulling her hair and telling her that she is repulsive, after which Kingston starts to cry as well.

Kingston suffers a strange illness but enjoys the next 18 months she spends in bed. When she returns to school, the quiet girl has not changed—she is still the perfect silent Chinese daughter. Kingston's shame at having humiliated the girl is just another secret she has to hide, along with the fact that her father is really a gambler and that many of her friends and neighbors are illegal, lying about their Communist affiliations. Secrets are seen as part of Chinese-American life, where children are raised by ghosts. Her mother keeps Chinese traditions alive but never explains them to her children. Kingston grows up thinking that if she ignores the traditions then the ghosts will not hurt her, and nothing bad will ever happen. She suspects that perhaps all the traditions are completely invented.

Kingston's parents talk about arranging her marriage. At a Chinese opera, Kingston hears a daughter character begging "beat me!" and understands that she is expected to be completely subservient to her future husband. She is worried that her parents will marry her off to a newly arrived immigrant. She also wishes she could tell her mother the secrets she has accumulated. She has a list of more than 200 things she would like to confess, from tormenting the quiet girl to her fantasies of being carried away by a white horse. Kingston attempts to tell her mother one secret every day, but her mother thinks she is unbalanced. Kingston is relieved not to have to confess anything else.

Kingston boldly decides she will not be a slave or a wife; she is planning on going to college. She also refuses to listen to her parents' illogical stories any longer. After making these assertions, she realizes she has just confessed several of the most important things from her list. Brave Orchid responds by saying Kingston is not as smart as she thinks she is. Why shouldn't she go to typing school? Kingston replies that she wants her mother to leave her and her sister alone and to stop arranging their marriages. Her mother calls her rude, especially to elders. Finally, Kingston asks why her mother always calls her ugly. Brave Orchid answers that it is the Chinese custom to say the opposite of what is true. Kingston leaves home to add simplicity and control to her life. She plans one day to visit China to see which of her parents' stories are true and which are mere inventions.

The last section of the book begins with Brave Orchid and ends with Kingston. Back in China, Brave Orchid's mother loved the theater and the entire family goes, despite the threat of bandits. They all remain safe. One of the performances tells the story of a female poet captured by a chieftain. She believes that the whine of the arrows is her captors' only music, until one night she hears them play the reed pipe. The poet is ransomed and married, and now her descendants sing "Eighteen Stanzas for Barbarian Reed Pipe" while playing their own instruments.

## Major Themes

*Woman Warrior* had a significant impact on the literary community in part because of its original style. Told as a mixture of fantasy, reported stories, and myths and legends, the book is less concerned with truth as fact and more with relating the feelings and emotional experiences associated with the situations it presents.

### Storytelling

Storytelling is a major theme in the book. Throughout, Kingston repeats stories her mother told her, tells many of her own, and also invents new endings for old tales. Storytelling is the method her parents used to pass the time and to impart their Chinese traditions and heritage. It is natural, thus, that Kingston would employ these same techniques and approaches when explaining her life to others. "I continue to sort out what's just my childhood, just my imagination, just my family, just the village, just movies, just living."

To Kingston, reporting or bearing witness is the same as avenging a crime. Like the woman warrior of the title, she carries her family's grievances with her, as well as her grievances about the way she was raised. By becoming a strong, independent, successful woman, she is breaking with the Chinese tradition of docility and achieving her own warrior status.

### The Role of Women

A secondary theme emerges in Kingston's criticism of how women are treated in Chinese culture. In this aspect of the work, Kingston lays as much of the blame on her mother as on her male relatives. Girls are seen as having little worth and no voice of their own. Kingston's mother cuts her daughter's tongue, ostensibly to loosen it, but an act that could also be interpreted as limiting her speech. Kingston is convinced that silence is akin to insanity, so she worries that her mother is confining her to a life of isolation and ostracism. She objects to the veil of silence that surrounds her aunt, punished for what should not have been a crime. Her living aunt accepts her husband's infidelity because she relies on him for financial support. By going to school and becoming a successful writer, Kingston breaks this silence, transforming it through her own critical voice.

## Truth Versus Fiction

Throughout the book, Kingston is concerned with the nature of truth. Her mother's stories bear little resemblance to any reality that Kingston recognizes, yet the delusions seem to be shared by her relatives and her community. The constant fear of ghosts and spirits, of ancestors and curses, haunts their lives and limits their possibilities. Kingston does not know what to believe. She has never been to China and so does not know how much of her parents' stories about the privations of life under Communism are true. As a result, she is afraid to go to China, afraid that she will disappear into one of the stories never to emerge again.

## Assimilation

The Chinese in Kingston's memoir do little to assimilate to American culture. They speak Chinese and send their children to Chinese schools. They treat their daughters as they have always done. Traditions are passed down, yet unexplained, so they seem like mysticism instead of heritage. Ultimately, Kingston's defense against the dysfunction and cultural isolation of her family is to break away from them, to attend college, and finally to speak out about her childhood. Her book represents her attempt to make sense of and to lay claim to her own often confusing past.

# AMY TAN

## Biography

AMY TAN should have been a doctor—or a concert pianist. That is what her parents, who immigrated to the United States from China in 1950, expected of her. Instead, she became a best-selling author.

Born on February 19, 1952, in Oakland, California, Tan grew up navigating two worlds—the traditional Chinese household in which she was raised and the American world outside her door. Tan received undergraduate and master's degrees in linguistics from San Jose State University and did graduate work at the Universities of California at Santa Cruz and Berkeley.

Amy Tan became a literary sensation in 1989 with the release of her novel *The Joy Luck Club*. It was a finalist for both the National Book Award and the National Book Critics Circle Award, as well as the recipient of many other honors and distinctions. In 1993, Wayne Wang directed the film version, and in 2007 the National Endowment for the Arts selected the novel for its "Big Read" program.

Tan is also the author of the novels *The Kitchen God's Wife, The Hundred Secret Senses, The Bonesetter's Daughter,* and *Saving Fish from Drowning*. She penned the memoir *The Opposite of Fate* and wrote two children's books, *The Moon Lady* and *Sagwa*.

Though Amy Tan writes mostly fiction, her novels are often based on her family history, which was marked by tragedy. She and her mother had a fraught relationship, a topic that she explores frequently in her work. Her mother witnessed Amy's grandmother's suicide (from an overdose of opium, a scene reimagined in *The Joy Luck Club*) and was raped before she left China. Her father and brother each died young from brain tumors, and Tan herself has suffered from severe and debilitating bouts of depression, for which she takes medication. Like her fictional character Jing-mei from *The Joy Luck Club*, Tan traveled to China to meet her half-sisters. "It was instant bonding," she said of the experience. "There was something about the country that I belonged to. I found something about myself that I never knew was there."

Her nonliterary endeavors include a stint as the narrator in the musical version of *Sagwa*, co-producer of the movie version of *The Joy Luck Club* (the screenplay of which she helped write), and author of the libretto for the San Francisco Opera's world premiere of *The Bonesetter's Daughter*. She is also lead rhythm, backup singer, and second tambourine in a literary garage band, the Rock Bottom Remainders. (A remainder is a book returned to the publisher by a bookstore that is unable to sell the leftover copies.) Her fellow band members include authors Barbara Kingsolver, Stephen King, Dave Barry, and Scott Turow. Tan is known for her rendition of "These Boots Are Made for Walking." The author-musicians perform annually for charity, benefiting literacy programs.

## *The Joy Luck Club*
### Summary and Analysis

*The Joy Luck Club* is a series of stories told by Chinese mothers and their Chinese-American daughters. There is a dual setting: modern-day San Francisco and the prewar China that the mothers remember. Each of the four sections is introduced by a parable that serves to illustrate the themes of that section and to tie the stories together.

The first section is "Feathers from a Thousand Li Away." Its parable is about a mother who bought a swan, in which she imbues all her hopes for her daughter: that she will be independent and happy, will speak perfect English, and know no hunger. But immigration officials take the swan away, leaving the woman with only a feather to show her daughter. Though the mother longs to explain to her daughter that she had always wanted the best for her, she waits until her English is perfect, a day that never comes.

Jing-mei or June is 36 years old when her mother dies and she is called to be the fourth player at her mother's monthly mah jong game. The Joy Luck Club, as her mother, Suyuan, called it, was a combination of a gaming society and an investment club (and the title of this chapter). June has grown up with her mother's stories of China during World War II. She was then the wife of an officer and suffered greatly, escaping Kwailin with only the clothes on her back. Before she dies, she reveals to June that she was married before and had two children she "lost" in the war. At the mah jong game, the other women hand June a check for $1,200. They have found her long-lost sisters in China and want her to go to meet them.

An-mei Hsu narrates the next section, "Scar," in which she tells of her mother, who left her parents' house in disgrace. The mother returns for An-mei and her brother, but a fight ensues, and An-mei is scarred by boiling soup.

In "The Red Candle," Lindo Jong is betrothed at the age of two to the son of a local family, the Huangs. Growing up, her mother treats her as though she already belongs to the other family. When the river floods her family's farm, she is sent to live with the Huangs until her marriage. Once in the household, she is treated as a servant and forced to respond to the spoiled son's every need. Finally, at sixteen she marries him, but they never consummate the marriage; her husband is still a child. Lindo's mother-in-law grows displeased and confines her to bed so that she will conceive a child, but the young woman never gets pregnant. Lindo knows she must escape her marriage and divorces with enough money to go first to Peking and then the United States.

The third member of the Joy Luck Club, Ying-ying St. Clair tells her daughter about the moon festival. Her family travels by boat, and Ying-ying accidentally falls out of the back. Fishermen pull her out of the water, and, believing her to be a beggar child, abandon her. She worries that she will never find her family again but is distracted by a play being performed. In it, the beautiful Moon Lady tells a sad story of greed and lust, which ends with her banishment to the moon. Fascinated, Ying-ying finds her after the play, wanting to make a wish. The Moon Lady, however, reveals herself to be a tired man in a wig and makeup, not a mythical figure after all. Saddened, Ying-ying is reunited with her family but never believes they "found the same girl."

In part 2, "The Twenty-Six Malignant Gates," the daughters speak. "Rules of the Game" is Waverly Jong's story. Daughter of Lindo Jong, Waverly is a chess champion in San Francisco. Originally motivated by her brothers' interest in the game, Waverly mastered the rules and strategies of the game. She becomes a protégé, featured at the age of nine in *Life* magazine and defeating opponents five times her age. Her mother reinforces the notion that Waverly is in charge of her own future, while simultaneously dictating that future through the enormous influence she exerts on her daughter.

In "The Voice from the Wall," Lena St. Clair, daughter of Ying-ying, tells of her mother's descent into mental illness. As a young mother, Ying-ying filled Lena's head with stories of evil men and monsters in the basement. As a result, Lena grows up scared. When Ying-ying gives birth to a stillborn baby, she believes it is punishment for the miscarriage she wished for in China. She reveals that she was a war bride whose age was changed at immigration, an alteration that makes her feel as though her entire identity was changed.

Lena is forced to translate for her mother but tells her father only good news, keeping Ying-ying's despair secret. Next door, Lena hears an Italian family through the walls; their knock-down, drag-out fights make her worry for the girl's safety. When the girl seeks sanctuary in Lena's room one night, only to sneak back into her own apartment via the fire escape, Lena sees that the fights reveal the bond and the love between mother and daughter, while her silent house merely reflects emotional distance and the absence of love.

In "Half and Half," Rose, the daughter of An-mei (who narrates the chapter "Scar"), is keeping the secret of her divorce from her mother. An-mei has never approved of Rose's marriage to Ted, a white man she met in college. Rose has a history of fearing her mother. When she was a child, tragedy struck the family on a trip to the beach. Rose was supposed to watch her younger brothers, but Bing disobeyed and was swept out to sea and drowned. Rose felt an overwhelming guilt, though her mother never blamed her. The loss of her son does, however, prompt the loss of An-mei's religious faith. Similarly, Rose lost her faith in love. She remembers when she first met Ted, but years later, a gulf has grown between them. What he sees as her Chinese passivity grates on him.

In "Two Kinds" we return to the narrator of the first chapter, Jing-mei (June), whose recently deceased mother was the founder of the Joy Luck Club. Jing-mei remembers her struggles with her mother as she was growing up. Her mother, desperate to escape the past and the babies she left behind in China, encourages Jing-mei to be a prodigy, deciding she will be a great pianist. In order to afford lessons, Suyuan cleans the teacher's house, which embarrasses Jing-mei. The young girl shows no natural talent at the piano and is mortified when, after her mediocre recital, Waverly says, "you aren't a genius like me." Afterwards, Jing-mei refuses to practice, saying to her mother, "You want me to be someone that I'm not!" The fight escalates. "I wish I wasn't your daughter." "Too late change this," Suyuan retorts. "Then I wish I were dead! Like them," Jing-mei responds, referring to the babies Suyuan left behind. With these final, stinging words, Jing-mei achieves her goal: She never has to play the piano again.

The third section of the book is called "American Translation." Lena St. Clair returns to narrate her part, "Rice Husband." She is anxious about her mother coming to visit her and her husband's new house. Her husband takes her for granted, ignoring the fact that she worked to establish his architecture firm. He insists they split all the bills down to the penny, when she makes much less money than he does. Her mother, of course, sees nothing but flaws in the new house, her indirect way of criticizing her daughter's unstable marriage, the frailty of which Lena is just beginning to recognize.

In a sequel to Waverly's earlier chapter "Rules of the Game," "Four Directions" takes up Waverly's adult life. She takes her mother to lunch at the Four Directions restaurant, planning to tell her that she is soon to be remarried, but never finds the opportunity to break the news, as Lindo prattles on about the poor service and the greasy food. Lindo disapproved of Waverly's first marriage, which ended in divorce, and Waverly indirectly blames her mother for its failure.

She brings her mother back to her apartment, where she is living with her fiancé, but her mother pretends not to notice. Waverly's reluctance to tell her mother she is marrying is understandable. "I had never known love so pure, and I was afraid that it would become sullied by my mother" and her criticisms. Waverly finally breaks the news to her mother, discussing Lindo's constant need to find fault as well. When Waverly and her fiancé postpone their honeymoon, after advice from the Joy Luck Club, until a season better suited for travel, Waverly imagines her mother accompanying them on the trip, "leaving our differences behind, stepping on the plane together, sitting side by side, lifting off, moving West to reach East" and thereby achieving integration.

"Without Wood" returns the reader to Rose's failing marriage. Now Ted wants a divorce, so he can remarry. Rose is devastated. She seeks advice from Lena, Waverly, her mother, even a psychiatrist, but cannot find peace. When Ted informs her that he wants her to hand over the house, she finally summons the will to stand up for herself and resist his controlling demands. She refuses to leave and returns the divorce papers unsigned. "You can't just pull me out of your life and throw me away," she says.

Jing-mei's low self-esteem is the subject of the next tale, "Best Quality," whose title refers to a jade pendant Jing-mei's mother, Suyuan, gave to her. The two go shopping for crabs to serve at Chinese New Year dinner, to which the Jongs are invited. At the gathering, the differences between the aggressive Jongs and the humble Woos become apparent. Lindo serves her daughter, Waverly, the best crab. Waverly makes fun of Jing-mei's haircut. Jing-mei responds, informing Waverly that her firm has never paid her for the freelance work she did for them. Waverly says Jing-mei was not paid because the work was substandard. Jing-mei again feels worthless and inferior.

After her mother's death, Jing-mei stands in her kitchen, cooking her father dinner. She finally comes to understand the significance of her mother's gift, realizing that, by giving Jing-mei the jade pendant, her mother was telling her that she was worth the "best quality" jade and that, sometimes, her mother was right.

The next section of the novel is "Queen Mother of the Western Skies." An-mei narrates the first chapter, "Magpies," relating a story that her mother once told her about how turtles turn humans' tears into magpies. An-mei thinks of her mother because she sees how much her daughter, Rose, is suffering in the wake of her divorce. Three generations of women have been victim to the inferior status imposed on the Chinese female.

An-mei met her mother when she was nine years old, when her mother came to claim her. She was known as a fallen woman, tricked into sleeping with a wealthy merchant, then forced to be his concubine. As fourth wife, An-mei's mother occupies the lowest position in the affluent household. She is so unhappy that she takes her own life by overdosing on opium. Her suicide gives An-mei the strength to resist the insincerity of the other wives. She justifies her mother's suicide. "That was China. . . . They had no choice. They could not speak up. They could not run away. That was their fate." Her mother sacrificed herself so that An-mei could have a better life. Back in the present day, An-mei wishes she could instill in her daughter that same urge to fight, to rebel.

"Waiting Between the Trees" presents a story the reader has heard before, but this time it is told from the mother's, Ying-ying St. Clair's, point of view. She is visiting her daughter Lena, where she sees how unhappy her daughter is in her marriage but laments her inability to honestly and directly tell her daughter so. Ying-ying describes her childhood, when she compared herself to a tigress, "waiting between the trees." Lena knows her mother was a poor war bride, rescued by Clifford St. Clair and brought to the United States; but Ying-ying had a life before the war.

A rich and beautiful woman, Ying-ying married a handsome flirt. The marriage soon soured, though, and her husband cheated on her. Becoming an abandoned wife, she believed she would never love again. She became the wife that she thought St. Clair wanted and assumed the role of a middle-class American, instead of a wealthy Chinese woman.

Now, in her daughter's guest room, she vows to summon her strength and regain her power as a tiger. "I will use this sharp pain to penetrate my daughter's tough skin and cut her tiger spirit loose. . . . I will win and give her my spirit, because this is the way a mother loves her daughter," she asserts.

"Double Face" takes as its plot a trip to Waverly's hairstylist so that Lindo can make a good impression on her in-laws. Waverly is conflicted about her Chinese heritage. On one hand, she embraces it, as it has become trendy to be "ethnic," but on the other hand, she is embarrassed by it. She is worried that when she goes to China on her honeymoon, they will not let her back into the United States. Her mother laughs this off, saying that Waverly is far too American for any Chinese person to believe she is a Chinese native as well. She also lacks the good qualities of a Chinese daughter: obedience, humility, and an ability to hide her true feelings.

Lindo remembers when she first arrived in the United States and met An-mei at the fortune cookie factory. She fell in love with her husband by reading fortunes. Because his background was so different, they did not share a language, even though they were both Chinese. They communicated in broken English and sign language. In proposing he asked her, "Will you spouse me?" Lindo thinks about the last time she went to China; people treated her as an American. She contemplates what she has given up to become American.

The last chapter in the book, "A Pair of Tickets," is a continuation of Jing-mei's story. Having discovered that her sisters are alive, she and her father go to China to see them and explain the reason behind her mother's actions. Jing-mei's name, in fact, means "long-cherished wish," and "little sister," indicating she was meant to find them.

Jing-mei and her father travel to her father's village. Rural China is very different from San Francisco, but Jing-mei is warmly accepted by her family. Her father finally tells her mother's story. Exhausted from fleeing Kweilin during the war, Suyuan set her twin daughters on the side of the road and went to look for food. She woke up days later in a refugee truck and was unable to find the girls, much less know if they were alive or dead.

The sisters fill in the missing parts of the story. They were rescued by a Muslim couple and raised in a loving home, still calling their absent mother "Mama."

Suyuan and her husband returned to China several times but were never able to find them. After her death, though, an old schoolmate of Suyuan's recognized the twins in a department store, as they looked so much like their mother.

Jing-mei and her father arrive in Shanghai and see her sisters. She does not immediately see the resemblance, but "they still look familiar. And now I also see what part of me is Chinese." In meeting her long-lost family, Jing-mei can finally come to accept and love her dual heritage.

## Major Themes

### The Mother-Daughter Relationship

Throughout the novel, the struggle between mothers and daughters is the primary theme. Though the mothers want the best for their daughters, their traditional Chinese values often clash with their daughters' American expectations. The older group of women expects obedience, humility, and docility from their daughters while simultaneously assuming they will have the confidence and opportunities of Americans. This struggle is manifested in the difficulties the older generation has in communicating with the younger.

Throughout the novel, the relationship between mothers and daughters is examined in all its complexity. The daughters gradually realize that their mothers are wise and correct in their judgment, and as much as they might fight the influence of their mothers, acting disobediently instead of dutifully, they still absorb their mothers' teachings. The mothers frequently understand their daughters better than the daughters understand themselves, though the mothers are often powerless to communicate this understanding. The daughters are undeniably influenced by their mothers, and their failure to understand and accept this part of themselves adds to the sense of alienation they experience as they struggle to forge their own individual identities. The daughters believe that they must be either Chinese or American, that one culture must be sacrificed to attain the other one. Gradually, by the end of the novel, they come to see that integration should be their goal.

### Gaps in Communication

The lack of communication found in the novel is due to, on its most basic level, language itself. None of the girls speaks adequate Chinese; none can read or write it. Their perfect American English gives the daughters an advantage and makes their mothers' speech sound rough and unpolished. The mothers are often given to telling parables, and the daughters dismiss these tales as superstition instead of recognizing the wisdom the tales impart. This language barrier also provides much of the humor in the novel. Tan has an incredible ability to mimic Chinese speakers of English with all their particular errors in grammar. Often the mothers' speech patterns sound harsh and critical, giving the reader an insight into how the daughters feel. Tan heightens this sense by often repeating stories from different points of view, so the reader can see how wide the chasm of perception is between the two generations.

Another source of the gap in communication in the novel can be traced to the mothers never sharing with their daughters the pain and suffering they experienced in the past, believing that sparing them will make them happier. The mothers have all faced great hardship, from losing children, to rape, to the suicides of their mothers. They have also been mistreated by men, a fate they hope to spare their daughters. However, the silence they adopt creates a gulf between them and their daughters. Only by relating the realities of the past, by dispelling the silence for good, can the gulf be mended.

Related to the characters' inability to fully know one another, the notion of appearance versus reality plays a major role in the book. The mothers are hiding their painful pasts, while the daughters pretend to be successful career women, mothers, and wives, while in truth they are unhappy and emotionally cut off. The need to pretend puts a strain on all the women. Part of this pressure stems from the split or bifurcated nature of the daughters' upbringing. They only become complete and happy when they are able to integrate their Chinese selves with their American lives.

### Assimilation and Cultural Influence

The daughters suffer from cultural dislocation. They are fully American yet have inherited the values and superstitions of their Chinese families. They do not feel fully accepted into American society but at the same time are distanced from their Chinese heritage. All marry white men and have trouble in their marriages, often stemming from cultural differences. The mothers see their daughters' unhappiness but can do nothing to remedy it.

The notion of assimilation is also a significant theme in the novel, as it is in much of immigrant literature. The daughters are influenced by and often caught between two worlds. The mothers constantly struggle with maintaining their culture and tradition in the face of American values. (It is telling that when Jing-mei goes to China, expecting to eat Chinese food, her family insists instead on eating hamburgers and apple pie.) The mothers uphold the traditions of the Joy Luck Club, the ties that bind them together, even though they are not blood relations. Rose, for example, seeks advice from Lena, Waverly, and Jing-mei when her marriage falls apart, though each offers very different insights. They potentially understand her upbringing better than her American friends do.

## *The Kitchen God's Wife*
### Summary and Analysis

*The Kitchen God's Wife* opens as Pearl, a young Asian American living in California, is called to a family gathering in honor of her cousin's engagement. She is reluctant to go; it is his fourth engagement, and her Chinese immigrant family exhausts her. When her Great Aunt Du dies—a relative of her mother's sister-in-law, Helen—Pearl and her husband attend the funeral with their two young daughters.

Helen's relationship with Pearl's mother, Winnie, is a mystery. They bicker like sisters but are not blood relations, yet seem held together by something more than just their co-owned flower shop. After the funeral, Helen issues Pearl an ultimatum: Either she tells Winnie that she was diagnosed with multiple sclerosis, or Helen will. Meanwhile, without Pearl's knowledge, Helen has given Winnie the same deadline: Confess her own secret by Chinese New Year or Helen will interfere.

Pearl and her mother have an equally fraught relationship. After the death of Pearl's father, they grew apart; Pearl chafed under the pressures of her duty as a daughter. Her mother's constant worrying and hovering felt oppressive, her circular logic impossible to overcome. Even in the present day, their relationship remains strained; Winnie does not approve of Pearl's white husband.

Auntie Du leaves Pearl a Chinese altar that Pearl finds ugly, but she decides her daughters can use it as a dollhouse. Winnie explains that the altar belongs to the Kitchen God. According to the story, a man named Zhang cheated on his wife and spent his fortune. He was reduced to begging in the street. One day, he sought shelter in a grand house. When he realized that it was his ex-wife's house, he jumped into the fire instead of staying to face her and his shame. Now he is known as the Kitchen God, and he reports back to heaven the actions of those here on earth.

At this point in the novel, the narrative switches to Winnie's point of view. She paints Helen as a know-it-all who has benefited from, but never recognized, her good luck, and she feels resentful that Helen bosses her around. Now Helen is making her tell all her secrets, beginning with the fact that Helen is not really Winnie's sister-in-law.

Winnie's story begins around 1920 in Shanghai, China, right before her mother abandons her. Her mother is the second wife of a rich merchant, a vain, beautiful woman who spoils Winnie, then known as Weiwei, her only child. Weiwei is never sure why her mother left, if she went to be with a man, if she was killed, if she merely became sick and died. All Winnie knows is that she is forced to leave her father's house to go live with her aunts and uncle on the island of Tsungming.

At her uncle's house, Weiwei is treated as a distant relation, second always to her plump cousin Peanut and the two younger boys. Peanut is a mischievous girl, and Weiwei is held responsible for her as her older "sister." The two go to the market around the new year, and Peanut pays a fortuneteller to reveal her future. The fortuneteller says she is to marry a local boy, and, seeing Peanut's disappointment, agrees to change her fortune for an additional fee. The fortuneteller then sees that Peanut will be rich and live in Shanghai. The woman also sees unhappiness in Weiwei's future, but before she can elaborate, Peanut insists they move on, leaving Weiwei to wonder what the fortuneteller might have done to alter her future too.

That day they meet Wen Fu, a charming young merchant, who sweeps them both off their feet. He seems to like Peanut; they kiss in the greenhouse and make Weiwei stand lookout. So Weiwei is surprised and glad, both for herself and because she can lord it over Peanut, when their families announce that Weiwei is to marry Wen Fu.

They travel to see Weiwei's father, whom she has not visited in 12 years. He reluctantly agrees to the marriage and tells his oldest wife to help Weiwei shop for her dowry, including ten pairs of silver chopsticks. Here the complicated rules of Chinese marriage customs become apparent. The groom's family offers a dowry, as though offering an estimate of what they think the daughter is worth. The bride's father then hands back the money on the wedding day "so you are not too much of a burden on your new family." Afterward, Weiwei realizes that her father has spent much less on her dowry than on that of her sisters.

Soon after the ceremony, Weiwei sees that her marriage is not what she had hoped. Still, she explains, "I was not always negative thinking, the way [Pearl] and Helen always say." Her new in-laws steal her dowry, selling the furniture as fake antiques to foreigners. Wen Fu is also not the honest businessman Weiwei thought. He neglects to tell her he joined the military, so she is surprised when he is called away to active duty in Hangchow. This is the first time she meets Helen, then called by her Chinese name, Hulan, who is married to a superior officer. Weiwei is confused. Helen's manners are coarse; she is uneducated and cannot read, and yet she was able to marry into a higher class.

Weiwei is uneducated, too, in the sense that she is innocent and naive. She believes a wife's duty is to "protect my husband so he would protect me. To fear him and think this was respect." So when he rapes and beats her, she believes this is part of her duty. By the time war breaks out between China and Japan, Weiwei is pregnant.

The men go off to fight in the war, leaving Weiwei "stuck in my dress, stuck in my marriage, stuck with Hulan as my friend." She begins to make the nature of her relationship with Hulan/Helen clear. "Maybe it's because we fought so much in those early days. Maybe it's because we had no one else to turn to. So we always had to find reasons to be friends. Maybe those reasons are still there." The wives are sent to Yangchow to wait for their husbands. After one week, they are forced to move again: the Japanese are coming. Nearly everyone in the regiment dies except Weiwei's husband, who guides his plane away from the fighting.

Weiwei is running out of money, so she wires Peanut to send her dowry money. She adds, "Hurry, we are soon *Taonan,*" a Chinese word meaning "doomed," after the telegraph operator urges her to exaggerate the importance. Wen Fu, however, uses the money to buy an overpriced car and then proceeds to crash it. Weiwei wires for more money with strict instructions that Peanut should send it only to her, but Nanking is bombed. Hulan and Weiwei avoid injury, but the war has officially started and the army moves again.

The two arrive in Kunming after a difficult journey, Weiwei eight months pregnant. Weiwei drops scissors, a sign of bad luck in China. Then Weiwei knocks over a table of scissors, and her luck turns even worse. The baby is stillborn. Wen Fu is injured, not in the fighting, but by stealing an army jeep and driving too fast. There is talk of a woman who was with him, and Hulan's husband does not prosecute him thanks to Hulan's interference.

Weiwei has a second baby, and Wen Fu abuses them both. One night, the baby becomes gravely ill. Weiwei goes to her husband, who is drunk and playing cards, and begs him to allow her to take the baby to the hospital. He refuses and says that she is exaggerating. When Weiwei returns with the dying child in her arms, it is too late, but Wen Fu tries to blame the death on her. All Weiwei can think is, "Good for you, Little One. You've escaped."

Weiwei is already pregnant when her daughter dies. She gives birth to a little boy, Danru. When she gets home from the hospital, she finds another woman in her bed. Hulan's Auntie Du has come to visit, and Weiwei hopes the sleeping woman is a relative, but she is, as Weiwei suspected, her husband's mistress. Instead of demanding that her husband get rid of the woman, though, Weiwei decides to accept her as a concubine, hoping that her husband will then leave her alone. She also likes the woman, who teaches her to dance. In return, Weiwei teaches her manners and gives her a stage name, Golden Throat, because she sings so well.

Weiwei begins to hatch a plan. Perhaps now that her husband has a mistress, he will agree to divorce her. She writes out a divorce writ, but her husband refuses to sign it. "When I want to divorce you, I will tell you. You don't tell me what to do." The next day, his mistress is gone.

The men leave again to fight, and the women endure a wave of bombings. Though Hulan and Weiwei constantly criticize each other, it is obvious that they depend on each other greatly. As Hulan is illiterate, she asks Weiwei to read a letter she has received, shamefully revealing that Hulan and her husband do not have a sexual relationship. That afternoon, they are separated in a bombing, and when they return home, Danru and Auntie Du are still missing. Weiwei goes out to look for them and sees a woman who has lost her son in the bombing. Weiwei promises to be a better wife, mother, and friend. The servants find her and reveal her son has returned home safely.

Wen Fu also returns home uninjured, and everyone attends an American dance. There, Weiwei dances and flirts with Jimmy Louie, an American-born Chinese man who works as a translator for the U.S. Army. This man, it is revealed, is Pearl's father. Weiwei and Jimmy have an instant connection, and Jimmy amuses her by giving them all American names: Weiwei becomes Winnie, and Hulan becomes Helen. Because Wen Fu is obnoxious, Jimmy names him Judas.

When they get home that night, Wen Fu is furious. He signs the divorce paper, then taunts her with the fact that she will never see her son again. The next morning, Auntie Du and Hulan refuse to sign the paper as witnesses. Still, Weiwei takes it and escapes, but Hulan, thinking she is helping, leads Wen Fu to where she is hiding. Weiwei is again subjected to Wen Fu's repeated abuse.

The war ends, and Hulan is sent back north. Wen Fu and Weiwei go to Shanghai. The women's parting is sad; despite their differences, they have become good friends, saved each other from death, and shared intimate secrets. They promise to keep in touch. Along the way, Weiwei sees the devastation wrought by the war: whole villages burned to the ground, people dead and missing. They go to her father's house in Shanghai to find it greatly changed. It is no longer a well-kept mansion but rather a rundown, ramshackle house, with graffiti such as "traitor" written on the walls. Her father's wife invites them in and offers them tea, explaining what happened. The Japanese occupied Shanghai and helped themselves to antiquities and businesses. Weiwei's father tried to resist; he even threw tea on a two-hundred-year-old scroll to make it worthless, but still the Japanese took everything, publishing his picture in the paper as praise for his cooperation. When the Japanese left, he was denounced as a traitor, and no one would do business with him anymore. He was ruined.

Weiwei goes to see him, but he has had a stroke and is catatonic; if he sees or hears her, he does not show it. Weiwei's hopes that her father will help her are dashed, as Wen Fu decides to strip the house of anything of value, including furniture that has been in their family for generations. Weiwei resolves to visit her aunts on the island she grew up on and then leave her marriage. To her surprise, when she arrives, they greet her warmly. Their family, too, has fallen on hard times. Her spoiled cousins are manual laborers. Even more surprising, Peanut has been divorced. She was tricked by the Communists, the aunts say. Though they say that Peanut is a terrible influence and that Weiwei should not try to visit her, they both secretly give Weiwei her address in Shanghai.

Weiwei goes to visit Peanut the following week, riding the bus to a seedy part of town. She lingers to look at a magazine, and a familiar voice calls her American name, Winnie. It is Jimmy Louis, who invites her to tea. He shows her a picture of the four sisters he is to choose one from to be his wife, but when they leave the teahouse, he leaves the picture on the table, proving his loyalty to Winnie. They agree to meet the following day, when he will escort her to Peanut's house. The next morning, Winnie is delayed by her demanding family. By the time she reaches their meeting place, she is nearly two hours late. Jimmy has waited for her. "We both stood in the road, our eyes wet with happiness, knowing without speaking that we both felt the same way."

Peanut lives in a rundown house. When Winnie arrives, she has a male visitor, who is helping her to paint slogans in her new role as a Communist activist. She has given up her former interest in clothes and makeup and laughs when she opens Winnie's present of stockings she has no use for. Peanut tells her story, claiming that her husband was a hermaphrodite, though she has proof only of his homosexuality. Depressed, Peanut went to visit their old school, where she was told of a former classmate's suicide. Little Yu's mother refused to help her daughter out of her terrible marriage, instead stressing duty and sacrifice. When Little Yu killed herself, her mother decided, "This was wrong, what happened to her, that she could find no other way, that she had no one to help her." She now dedicates her life to helping other women escape their marriages and runs the house that Peanut lives in as a hideout for runaway wives.

Winnie plans to take her son and escape her marriage. Yet she feels terrible about betraying her invalid father. She goes to see him, to explain herself, even if he is too ill to hear her. To her surprise, he manages to communicate the fact that there are three gold pieces hidden in the rod at the base of the scroll he ruined to prevent the Japanese from taking it. Armed with the gold, Winnie claims she is going to visit her aunt, who is in ill health. She moves in with Jimmy Louis instead. Together they live as husband and wife and raise Danru as their child. Winnie sues for divorce, hiring a lawyer with the gold pieces and claiming that she was divorced during the war when her husband held a gun to her head to make her sign the document. Wen Fu arranges to have the lawyer's office ransacked and the divorce paper destroyed.

Two men come by looking for Winnie. Scared, she sends Danru to stay with Hulan. She remains, needing to be in Shanghai when the divorce comes through. Auntie Du then arrives unannounced. Winnie senses right away that Danru has died; both he and Hulan's husband have succumbed to a plague spread by rats. Winnie is devastated, but before she even has time to grieve, she is arrested and taken to jail. Accused of taking her husband's property and his son, of neglecting Danru and causing his death, and of running off with an American soldier, with no divorce paper to clear her name, she is sentenced to two years in prison. Wen Fu gives her one chance to return to him. "I would rather sleep on the concrete floor of a jail than go to that man's house."

The newspapers make a scandal of the divorce, printing lies about both parties. Jimmy has to return to the United States. There is no way he can help her out of jail. He writes her often, then less often. He has become deeply religious and writes of his love for God. Winnie's father dies, telling Wen Fu in a moment of deathbed lucidity that there is gold hidden in the house. Wen Fu tears the house down in a futile effort to discover it. In jail, Winnie teaches her fellow inmates, just as she did her father's concubine those years ago. She reads in the newspaper that Wen Fu's former concubine has committed suicide after gaining moderate success as Miss Golden Throat. Winnie decides to take action. She sends Jimmy a telegram asking if she can come to the United States and be his wife.

Auntie Du and a newly remarried and pregnant Hulan come to visit Winnie in jail. Hulan is married to an important official who claims that he can get Winnie out of jail. True to his word, Winnie is released early, but Hulan's husband seems embarrassed by her gratitude. Then, Auntie Du reveals that she was the one who went to the officials and claimed that Winnie was related to an important Communist who would punish those who imprisoned his relation. Auntie Du and Winnie never reveal this to Hulan. Still, it is the favor that Hulan holds over Winnie and the reason Winnie sponsors Helen and her husband's immigration.

Mother and son slide into poverty until Winnie remembers that she has hidden her ten pairs of silver chopsticks in her suitcase. It is enough to keep them afloat. Winnie goes to the telegraph office to tell Jimmy the news and ask him what she should do. The telegram operator recommends she add the words, "Hurry, soon we are *Taonan*." Winnie recognizes the old phrase and the same woman who helped her back when the war started. Jimmy sends a response saying that Winnie's papers have come through and that she should leave for the United States immediately.

First, Winnie wants a divorce. She sends Wan Fu a telegram saying that there is an important package for him, but that he must come with his wife, for it requires both signatures. When he arrives with his mistress, the telegraph operator says that she recognizes him from the newspaper and that the woman he is with is not his wife. Wen Fu insists that he divorced Winnie years before, when Winnie emerges from her hiding place and produces witnesses. Under pressure from his mistress, Wen Fu signs the document releasing Winnie from the marriage.

Wen Fun gets his revenge, though, finding her one night, raping her at gunpoint, and stealing her plane tickets. Winnie manages to get the gun and fires it at him, causing a flesh wound. Hulan, hearing the noise, comes to the room. She helps Winnie recover her plane tickets and throw Wen Fu's pants out the window. He leaves the house humiliated. Winnie leaves for the United States soon afterwards, discovering almost immediately that she is pregnant.

The narrative then switches back to Pearl's point of view. She believes that her mother is trying to tell her that she is Wen Fu's child, the daughter of her mother's rape, but Winnie claims she does not know who Pearl's biological father is. She worried throughout Pearl's childhood that she would display signs of Wen Fu's bad temper, this excessive concern explaining some of Winnie's strict and harsh attitude toward her daughter. Winnie tells Pearl that she felt she had to keep her former life a secret, otherwise Pearl would think she was a bad mother. After looking for years for signs that Pearl takes after one man or the other, Winnie decides that her daughter looks just like all the other children she had and lost. Above all, Pearl is her daughter. Pearl meets her mother's words with her own confession, telling her mother about her multiple sclerosis.

Helen is contented; she considers Pearl and Winnie's new closeness a direct result of her meddling. She insists on going to China to look for medication for her "brain tumor," an invented condition that no one believes she actually has. In truth, Helen reveals to Pearl, they are going for Pearl's sake, to look for Chinese medicines to cure her. She wants to help Pearl because, "All those years, I forgot to thank your mother. What a good friend your mother is."

The last chapter is told from Winnie's point of view. She confesses that Helen reveals to her that both she and Auntie Du knew that Wen Fu was Pearl's father. Helen apologizes for always downplaying the extent of Wen Fu's evil and vicious ways, explaining that she did not want Winnie to blame Pearl for her father's abusive nature.

Winnie buys Pearl a new idol to put in the altar that Auntie Du left her. Instead of the Kitchen God, Winnie buys an irregular nameless figure, rejected by the factory, and gives it the name Sorrowfree. Though she dismisses it as a harmless superstition, still she encourages Pearl to admire the smoke from the incense as it curls upward.

## Major Themes

### Secrets and Confessions

One of the major themes of *The Kitchen God's Wife* is the keeping and telling of secrets. Both Pearl and Winnie keep secrets from each other, which only serves to weaken their relationship. Winnie and Helen have their own secrets, too, often painful confessions they keep to themselves and allow to fester through the years. It is only after Helen's decision that she wants to face her first husband in heaven with a clean conscience that the truth is revealed. The secrets are shameful but also function as a bond between the women. When the secrets are told, when the truth each woman protected for so long is finally revealed, the bonds only strengthen. Friendship and love prove more powerful and enduring than secrecy and shame.

### The Abuse of Women

Another major component of the novel is the violence, abuse, and intimidation the women are forced to endure. Tan depicts women in pre-revolutionary China as nearly worthless, valued only for their beauty and their ability to give birth to sons. They have nearly no control over their lives or any hand in shaping their present or future. Weiwei is unable to divorce Wen Fu, even though he abuses her. Even if she escapes the marriage, there is nowhere for her to go. No one will help her or take her in, viewing her as disgraced for wanting to escape such vicious treatment. Suicide becomes a grim, desperate option for those women who can imagine no other course. Weiwei never finds out what became of her mother, who chafed at her role as a second wife and longed for luxuries her husband could not provide.

For Helen and Winnie, then, the United States is not necessarily a place they seek out in order to pursue the American Dream but a safe and distant refuge free from abuse and injustice. It is love that allows Winnie to come to the United States, and her debt to Helen that brings Helen and her husband to the new land too. Once the basic need for safety and protection from violence is realized in these women's lives, the families are able to embrace their part of the American Dream, achieving financial independence and raising assimilated children.

## Chinese History and Culture

World War II is the setting for the bulk of the novel. The characters in the novel do not question China's involvement, nor do they support it. There are no Japanese characters in the novel. Though the Japanese bomb and occupy China, they are merely another enemy in the characters' lives. Similarly, when the Communists take over China, Winnie and Helen are neither glad nor unhappy. Their desire is to survive, and they will do whatever it takes to survive to the end of the war. Similarly, Winnie accepts her jail sentence with stoicism, waiting patiently for her time there to end.

Still, the values and customs of China remain, from the superstitions to the complicated rules involving hospitality and gifts. The negative thinking that both women criticize each other for displaying also endures. "She sees something good—her children acting nice—she thinks something bad. . . . Isn't that negative thinking, to think you are going to die because everyone is nice? We have the same expression in Chinese, *daomei* thinking. If you think *daomei, daomei* will happen." It is an inverted and complicated means of protecting one's self from tragedy and disappointment, to assume and prepare for the worst so that, then, the good will come as a pleasant surprise. As many characters believe in the novel, to feel that you are lucky invites the gods to punish you.

This circular thinking is a source of frustration for the characters but is also a source of humor. Helen complains that her daughter calls her "for no reason," which is really a way of subtly bragging about their close relationship and criticizing Winnie's strained relations with Pearl. Winnie, in turn, finds it amusing that Helen and her daughter, in all their closeness, spend ten minutes arguing about how expensive long-distance telephone calls are. Helen then convinces her daughter to hang up the phone, as a way of reminding herself of her daughter's continued obedience: "See? She still listens to me." This notion of raising daughters to be obedient, in the face of an American emphasis on independence, displays the strength and endurance of Chinese culture and tradition, which values filial duty. Duty in all its forms, to friends and family, is a primary motivating factor in the novel. Duty must be upheld; the characters do not feel they have a choice.

## Luck and Destiny

Luck and destiny are also major themes in the novel. Winnie believes strongly that luck and fate can be altered and influenced. She accuses Peanut of interfering with her fortune and thus changing the course of her life. She tells Jimmy that their meeting, which would prove to be her salvation in the future, is merely luck. Throughout her life, people from Winnie's past return, and, in the case of the telegraph operator, prove to be crucial allies. Though her life is filled with tragedy, she still recognizes that she is better off than many others. Before they immigrate, Helen envies Winnie's ability to have children, even if they come from an abusive and unloving marriage.

The Kitchen God of the title is a symbol of luck, but it also carries associations of revenge and injustice. The god is a man who mistreated his wife. Rather than admit he was wrong, he kills himself by jumping into fire. Even then, his wife, bound by kindness and duty, tries to put out the flames. Instead of being punished in the afterlife, he is assigned to report on people's actions. Despite this seeming male privilege, women still worship him, so he will curry favor for them with the more important gods. When Winnie buys a replacement god for the altar at the end of the book, she is breaking the cycle of female subjugation and passivity and assuming control by creating her own form of luck instead.

# GISH JEN

## Biography

GISH JEN was born Lillian Jen in 1956 in New York. She took the pen name Gish Jen after her namesake, actress Lillian Gish. Born to immigrant parents, Jen lived her earliest years in Yonkers, just north of New York City. The family then moved to Scarsdale (thinly veiled as Scarshill in *Mona in the Promised Land*), a more affluent upper-class suburb.

Jen describes discrimination in her early years, having rocks thrown at her and taking judo to learn to defend herself. The move to Scarsdale ended the violence but not the sense of "otherness" she felt. Hers was a strict Chinese household. Her mother came from a wealthy family and was sent to the United States to be educated before marriage. Her father came to the United States as a hydraulics engineer to help with the war effort. Both were essentially stranded in their new country, when the Communists took over China and the U.S. government refused to let them leave.

Jen attended Harvard University, graduating in 1977 with a B.A. in English literature. She then worked in the fiction department of publishing house Doubleday, before enrolling in Stanford Business School. She left after her second year, without a degree, to travel to China, where she was an English instructor at a coal-mining institute. While in China, she decided to try her hand at writing and returned to the United States to attend the prestigious Writers' Workshop at the University of Iowa. She received her M.F.A. in 1983.

Jen published *Typical American* to great acclaim in 1991, but she was already well-known for her stories. "Birthmates" was chosen by John Updike for inclusion in *Best American Stories of the Century*. Her other books include *Mona in the Promised Land* (1996); the collection of stories, *Who's Irish* (1999); and *The Love Wife* (2004). She has taught at Tufts, the University of Massachusetts, Radcliffe, and

Harvard and is currently the co-director of the Brandeis University creative writing department. Her many honors include a National Book Critics Circle Award nomination for *Typical American*, a National Endowment for the Arts grant, and the Mildred and Harold Strauss Living from the American Academy of Arts and Letters, in 2003, which awards $50,000 a year for five years. She was elected to the American Academy of Arts and Sciences in 2009 and currently lives outside Boston, Massachusetts, with her husband and two children.

## *Mona in the Promised Land*
### Summary and Analysis

Mona Chang is in middle school when her Chinese immigrant parents move from their house in the city of New York to the wealthy enclave of Scarshill in the nearby suburbs. Mona is the only Asian in her class, entertaining her new friends with false tales of Chinese exoticism and her martial arts prowess. That distinction changes when Sherman Matsumodo, a newly arrived Japanese student, enrolls at Mona's school. Everyone assumes that Mona can communicate with him, despite the longstanding animosity that exists between China and Japan. Tentatively, they begin to date, holding hands but not kissing until his last day in the United States, when, their parents enacting an overly formal tea party, the couple escapes to the bushes behind the house. Sherman kisses her neck, but the intimacy does not last long, as they suddenly start fighting. Sherman uses his martial arts ability to flip her onto the ground. She later writes him long letters, but he responds with a sole sentence: "You will never be Japanese."

Meanwhile, Mona increasingly absorbs the practices of her Jewish classmates. Her best friend, Barbara Gugelstein, decides at the age of 16 to renew her faith, and Mona goes with her to synagogue. She peppers her speech with Yiddishisms like "oy!" when she is not pretending to talk like her immigrant parents, who are different from Barbara's parents. Mona's mother, first of all, thinks that it is "no good for a girl to be too smart anyway." Second, it is obvious that, to Mona's mother, "women distinguish themselves in life by their misery." Third, the Changs own a pancake house, where Mona is expected to help out on weekends. Barbara's family, on the other hand, emphasizes education; her father is an executive.

Mona's older sister, Callie, starts attending Harvard University, where her roommate is black, which somewhat shocks her parents. Now Mona is alone with her parents and ardently wishes for Callie's return. Callie, in turn, hears that Mona is converting to Judaism and tells their parents. "What kind of daughter lies to her mother?" Mona's mother asks. Mother and daughter begin to fight over everything, including Mona's winter jacket, which her mother throws away. When Mona retrieves it and places it on the radiator to warm, it burns a hole, causing the down jacket to burst. Mona and her mother are united in ridding the house of the down feathers. They offer an even more united front when the mailman arrives, claiming they are completing a science project for school. "Shaming your family" is the worst possible sin in the Chang household.

Mona complains to the rabbi and to the other youth in the "rap sessions" that her parents do not believe they are a minority group, despite the fact that the "Chinese are the new Jews." They have raised her to be American but cling to Chinese customs and notions of filial duty.

Mona and Barbara start volunteering at the youth crisis center hotline. Though they suffer the usual ups and downs of adolescent friendship—Barbara becomes friends with the popular Eloise—they remain close, so close that it is not immediately apparent which one of them Seth Mandel is interested in. It soon becomes clear that he is fascinated by Mona, a Chinese Jew. Mona rejects him, and he turns his attentions to Barbara, disappearing into the utility closet with her to do "who-knows-what." Mona quickly switches from her Chinese-immigrant impersonation to her Yiddish grandmother voice: "What am I, chopped liver, you should do this to me?" Barbara tells Mona that she had her chance, and Mona swallows her jealousy.

Barbara moves to a large new house, and the girls bravely explore what they believe to be a stop on the Underground Railroad but what actually turns out to be a wine cellar. Barbara loses her virginity and suspects she is pregnant, but Seth wants to have an open relationship. Mona struggles with complicated feelings of jealousy and inadequacy. Compared to Barbara, her body is undeveloped and childlike. "Your legs are not your problem," her mother says. Meanwhile, a Japanese boy matching Sherman's description calls the hotline. Could it really be Sherman? When Barbara, relieved to find out she is not pregnant, gets on the phone to listen in, she says she suspects it is not Sherman but a male friend of theirs playing a joke. After one call, Sherman hangs up, saying, "You will never be Japanese." Barbara feels terrible at having been wrong and gives Mona her van for the summer to make it up to her. They celebrate with banana splits at Mona's parents' pancake house, enjoying themselves until Barbara sees that Andy Kaplan, her longtime friend and potential love interest, is dating Eloise.

One summer day, Mona is driving Barbara's van when she is surprised by Seth, who was taking a nap in the back. Apparently, Barbara left them both the keys. He continues to drive the van, even though Mona parks it in her driveway. One evening, Mona hears Seth in the driveway. She goes out to confront him and is grabbed by an assailant she assumes to be Seth. It isn't Seth, however, and it is clear the man is trying to assault her. Luckily, Seth is there, an "avenging angel" who scares off her attacker with his bicycle pump.

Mona cannot tell her parents about the incident, because her mother did not want her to keep the van in the first place and would disapprove of her sneaking outside at night. Instead Mona confides her anxiety to Seth, who tries to soothe her with a kiss. Soon, their newfound intimacy amounts to more than just kissing. Seth lives in a teepee in his parents' yard. In an attempt to be radical and nonconventional, he has decided not to go to college and disparages the activism his stepmother performs. He also continues his education of Mona, forcing her to see art films. "He gives her a book, *Notes from the Underground*. This, it turns out, is not exactly *Love Story*."

Barbara has had rhinoplasty and returns from vacation still swollen from her nose job. Seth calls her vain, but Mona, in an attempt to help her make the change less noticeable, suggests bangs. While sharing a sundae at the pancake house, Mona tells her about Seth. Barbara does not seem to mind. Instead, she is still upset that Andy Kaplan is dating Eloise.

Seth and Barbara begin to work at the pancake house, bringing a new racial mix to the employees. Cedric, the manager, is Chinese, while all the cooks are black. Barbara, Seth, Mona, and Alfred, the cook, discuss the Black Power movement and compare the tribulations of their different minority groups. They become friends, and when Alfred gets kicked out of his girlfriend's apartment because he was cheating on her, Mona decides that he should move into Barbara's garage, using the wine cellar to travel in and out so that no one knows he is living there. Barbara says he should live in the main house but needs to be careful not to tell Evie, her cousin, who is studying photography and living in the otherwise empty house, as Barbara's parents are away for the summer.

Alfred becomes less and less quiet and less and less grateful. He wants to watch television, listen to music, and have friends over. Evie almost discovers his presence on more than one occasion. Finally, Barbara and company decide to tell Evie, but she is busy printing photographs, so the moment passes.

Mona goes to visit Callie at the resort she is working at in Rhode Island. Callie's roommate Naomi explains that they are all "involuntarily stuck to one another . . . by virtue of their being colored folk." Mona has never thought about her ethnic origins in such a way. Eloise and her parents arrive at the resort, which creates an awkward tension.

When Mona returns, she suspects that Barbara and Seth have started seeing each other again, though they deny it. Then, a crisis erupts. The friends discover that Alfred is throwing a party in the living room and that Evie is sitting on his lap. She has been having an affair with him all summer.

As the summer ends, Alfred and Evie break up. Barbara's mother finds Evie's photos and discovers their summer activities. Evie is sent home; Alfred is fired. Barbara's mother tells her she is too Jewish. She also informs her daughter they have sold her van and that her father's job is in jeopardy. When Mona breaks up with Seth, to her surprise, he begins to cry and tells her he loves her.

Mona begins to receive phone calls from Sherman, who has moved to the United States and learned English. They speak philosophically of cultural difference, but he is still skittish and hangs up whenever the call gets too personal. Seth packs up his teepee and goes to college. Alfred sues the pancake house for racial discrimination, and in the ensuing fight with her parents, Mona threatens to run away. When her mother slaps her, Mona becomes convinced that leaving her family is the only solution.

Mona takes the train to New York City, where she runs into Seth's stepmother. She decides to go stay with Callie at Harvard, but when she arrives, Callie and her roomate have gone on a trip. Mona adopts Callie's life, staying in her room and wearing her clothes. When her mother calls, Mona pretends to be her sister. She tells her mother that Mona has gone to France to go to the beach *topless*, a word her mother does not know. Her mother says that it is not fair to run away, that if Mona wants to leave home, she should wait for her parents to kick her out.

The phone rings again and, to Mona's surprise, it is Sherman Matsumoto. He apparently talks to Callie frequently and is worried about Mona's disappearance. Mona's mother calls again but refuses to admit that she wants Mona to come home.

One day, Mona hears a familiar voice on the other side of the door. Sherman has come to see her. Mona opens the door to find Seth. He apologizes, then explains. It was originally Andy Kaplan who had called the hotline as a joke. When Andy abandoned the prank, Seth resumed the calls. Mona is angry but forgives him. They are in bed when Mona's parents show up. Embarrassed, the Changs quickly leave.

Mona decides she has missed too much school in her senior year and wants to return. She and Seth return to Scarshill but do not know where to live. Mona cannot go home, and if they camp out in Seth's teepee, Mona's parents will find out she is in town. Barbara, then, comes up with an idea. Because her father is out of work, the family has moved back into the old, smaller house. The new house is on the market. Mona and Seth hide there. One night, a burglar breaks in. They discover it is a former employee at the pancake house who was fired. They wonder if he was Mona's attacker as well. The burglar is carrying Barbara's father's flask, which they had accused Alfred of stealing, so they go to Alfred's house to apologize and ask him to drop the suit against Mona's father. He agrees and says he is back in touch with Evie.

Mona goes home to tell her parents the good news about the lawsuit, but she finds her mother disheveled, in her bathrobe in the middle of the day. Her mother turns away from her to return to her room.

In the epilogue, Mona is "sort of married to Seth; they're going to be more married soon" in a ceremony that makes their common-law marriage legal. Celebrating with them will be their daughter, Io. Barbara, married not once but twice to Andy Kaplan, will be the maid of honor. Callie has become a pediatrician, fulfilling their parents' desire for their daughters to be doctors. Someone had to, she explains. "It would have killed Mom if we'd both been like you."

Mona wonders if it is possible that her rebellious spirit and actions will kill her mother. She has not spoken to her mother in years. She had thought the birth of her daughter would bring them together, and even planned to name her daughter after her mother if she came to visit the baby, but only her father showed up.

On the day of Mona's wedding to Seth, however, the door opens to reveal Mona's mother. Io falls down in her excitement but rights herself, and the novel ends with the little girl clapping.

# Major Themes

## Parent-Child Relations

Mona's most difficult relationship is with her mother. Her mother constantly criticizes her and refuses to accept that Mona is an American. Her mother expects perfect obedience and docility, but Mona is a smart, independent young woman. In this manner, her mother represents Mona's Chinese heritage tugging at her. Though Mona fits in with her Jewish friends and uses the Torah for moral guidance, her mother's constant disapproval is a symbol of her alienation from her native culture.

## The Multicultural World

Mona navigates a complicated world. She is ethnically Chinese but adopts Judaism as her religion. Throughout the novel, these worlds constantly collide, providing friction and conflict that only time will resolve.

Mona assimilates so thoroughly into the culture of Scarshill that she adopts the Yiddish-inflected English of her friends. This mode of speaking provides much of the humor in the novel. Between her mother's broken English and misheard words, Mona and Barbara's Yiddish-inflected shorthand, and Alfred and his friends' Black Power slogans, Jen's mimicry of ethnic speech patterns is both realistic and funny. Beneath the comedy, however, lies the lack of understanding that separates these various groups and cultures and the complicated feelings of guilt and forgiveness the divisions create.

Throughout the novel, Jen is able to comment on the idea of race in America. There are many types of Americans represented. Mona's parents are successful immigrants but are cut off from the rest of society. Their black employees are treated as inferior and are easily fired. Mona exists at the center of the novel's various racial and cultural conflicts. She considers Chinese immigrants to be "the new Jews." It is ironic that, in the world of Jen's novel, the minority Jews are the dominant culture to which Mona is drawn. She has even assimilated the guilt that some white Americans feel toward African Americans and racist behavior and attitudes in general.

Mona's parents can be considered the victims of their own success. They have raised an American daughter, headstrong and curious, independent and freethinking. However, it is this same culture that makes Mona unable to live up to her parents' expectations. She does not marry until after she has had a child. It is this daughter, the next generation of an American family, who finally brings the women together.

# HA JIN

## Biography

THOUGH HE WRITES exclusively in English, Ha Jin is a native Chinese speaker who did not live in an English-speaking country until the age of 29. He was born Xuefei Jin in 1956 in a remote province of northern China to a military officer and his wife. He joined the People's Liberation Army at 14 and served on the border between China and what was then the Soviet Union. After leaving the army, he became a railroad telegrapher in a small town. He worked the night shift and taught himself high school courses, including English, hoping to read a seminal Marxist text by Friedrich Engels in that language.

Caught in the throes of the Cultural Revolution, Ha Jin did not have the opportunity to attend college until institutions of higher learning reopened in 1977. Because he had never had a formal education, he did not perform well on his entrance exams and was fortuitously assigned to his last choice of major: English. He went on to earn his master's degree in the subject.

In 1985, he traveled to the United States for the first time on a scholarship to Brandeis University outside Boston, Massachusetts. He had always intended to return to China, but the Tiananmen Square uprising in 1993 made him realize he could never go back to live in his homeland. He remained in the United States instead, where he supported himself and his wife by working as a night watchman in a factory, leaving his son with his grandparents in China. He began to write in English, the language whose literature he had loved, and took the pen name Ha Jin, which he found easier for Americans to pronounce. He earned his Ph.D. in1993 and was subsequently hired by Emory University in Atlanta, Georgia.

His first book, the poetry collection *Between Silences*, was published in 1990. To date, he has published two other books of poetry (*Facing Shadows* and *Wreckage*), four short story collections (*Ocean of Words: Army Stories*, *Under the Red*

*Flag, The Bridegroom,* and *A Good Fall*), five novels (*In the Pond, Waiting, The Crazed, War Trash,* and *A Free Life*) and a book of essays (*The Writer as Migrant*). He has won an array of major writing awards, including the PEN/Hemingway Award, the Flannery O'Connor Award, the National Book Award, and the PEN/ Faulkner Award, among others. Currently, he teaches at Boston University.

## *War Trash*
### Summary and Analysis

*War Trash* is the story of a Chinese soldier held prisoner during and after the Korean War. The first-person narrator tells his tale while vacationing in the United States, where his American granddaughter discovers his secret: a tattoo on his stomach that explicitly denounces the United States. This discovery prompts Yu Yuan to write his long-planned memoir, after which he plans to return to China where he will end his days.

His story begins in Chengdu, China. After graduating from a prestigious military academy, he is assigned to the 180th Division of the People's Liberation Army, a unit noted for its resistance to the Japanese invasion during World War II. He is stationed near his widowed mother and close to his fiancée, Julan. He admires the Communists for doing away with corruption and establishing order in China.

In 1951, his unit is posted to Hebei, where the men prepare to enter Korea, amid worries that the U.S. Army plans to invade northern China. The unit is assigned Russian arms that they are unable to operate, but Yuan is not worried. He knows some English, is a clerical officer, and most likely will not see action.

The army begins to march along the Yalu River. Yuan admires his superior, Commissar Pei Shan, who frequently, on the 400-mile walk to the 38th Parallel, calls him into his jeep to translate English documents.

Many of Yuan's misconceptions are overturned by his eyewitness account. He sees how poor the Korean countryside is and marvels at the extent of the destruction. He meets many Chinese laborers, who communicate with Koreans in basic Japanese. Some Koreans are sympathetic; others spy for the Americans. It is impossible to tell where allegiances lie.

Yuan has misgivings about the military's strategy. The army begins its fifth offensive directly after the fourth, though the men are exhausted and the equipment inferior. The offensive goes well. The soldiers wonder why there was no American retaliation. The officers, unable to issue orders unless told to by the higher-ranking officials, are powerless, and the army stays marooned in enemy territory. In that time, the supply line collapses, and when the Americans begin the counterattack, the men are trapped. Conflicting orders confuse them, and they attempt to ford the river, swollen from recent rain. The ill-planned crossing costs lives and what little supplies the men have left. They are cut off from food and water and endure extreme hunger and thirst.

Again, conflicting orders arrive via telegram. The officers discuss their options. Commissar Pei says they should take into account the situation on the ground, which the higher-ranking personnel could not possibly know, but the other officer stresses that they must obey orders. Therefore, the army does not press its position, losing any advantage it might have had. "We were like hungry ghosts," Yuan notes, "fearful but unable to stop wandering around." Unsurprisingly, many of the men desert.

As Yuan walks, wounded men beg him and Commissar Pei to be taken with them. Over the next three months, while the men desperately search for food and try to wage guerilla warfare, the company is reduced to 34 men. At one point, the men are so desperate, they butcher the rotten corpse of a horse.

The bedraggled company comes across another field unit, which has some grain to share. Commissar Pei is suffering from an ulcer but can eat the porridge, and the men's morale improves. They consider surrender, but army officials have convinced them that the United States would use them as guinea pigs for biochemical testing, and so they prefer to fight to the death.

The men come across a band of terrified civilians cooking a large pot of rice, but communication barriers prevent them from talking or sharing the food. In another village, they find a cache of rice. Pei leaves an IOU in its place; army regulations insist that they must not steal from villagers. Yuan passes the time by reading *Uncle Tom's Cabin* with the help of his dictionary. The troops marvel at how well American slaves eat. Yuan attempts to teach the men some English. His friendship with Pei grows—they are both educated, which sets them apart from most of the men.

One day, they are attacked. A grenade goes off, and Yuan later wakes up in the back of a jeep. His leg is numb, though it appears that the rumors of American soldiers castrating prisoners are untrue. He is ashamed to be alive; the instructions were to kill yourself if captured by the enemy. Unwilling and unable to do so, Yuan decides to lie to his captors. He wishes they had killed him.

Yuan finds himself in a prisoner of war hospital in Pusan, the provisional capital of South Korea. His left thigh was badly injured by shrapnel, so he is excused from interrogation. Yuan lies to the registration officials, saying that his name is Feng Yan, and that he is a new recruit who speaks no English. His first operation goes well, though it is clear that the American surgeons are medical students with little experience. In his pain and confusion, he almost speaks English.

The hospital is run by Chinese collaborators, who will not be able to return to China and who care little about their countrymen. The patients rely on one another for nursing care. Yuan is glad to see Ding Wanlin from his division, who helps him. The rest of the hospital tent is filled with men with a hodgepodge of injuries. There are no painkillers, and the men rant deliriously. One patient has maggots eating his wound. Yuan begins to worry about his own wound, which is healing badly. There is another piece of shrapnel in his leg, and he needs a second operation. He refuses to let the student-doctor operate on him, speaking English in his panic, which reveals to the men that he is educated, probably an officer.

He makes such a fuss that they call a doctor who speaks perfect Mandarin, Dr. Greene, a white woman who grew up in China with her missionary parents. Yuan is smitten. He shows her how to write Chinese characters in calligraphy.

Now able to move around on crutches, Yuan explores his surroundings. He runs into Commissar Pei, who goes by the alias Wei Hailong, or "Old Wei." He has heard of Yuan's closeness with Dr. Greene and encourages him to get to know her better, so as to glean information from her. One day, Dr. Greene informs Yuan that he will be transferred to Koje Island. She writes him a note excusing him from work, and they part.

Yuan arrives at an immense prison camp run by pro-Nationalists (those who oppose Communist rule in China). Yuan's heart sinks. The Nationalists want to return to Taiwan when the war is over, to avoid Communist China, and they pressure everyone into registering as Taiwanese. The enforcement group places him in a shabby tent with others who are Communists, or, more realistically, men who simply want to go home. It is so crowded that the men lie on top of one another to sleep. They are given only half a bowl of boiled barley, while the officers eat well, a marked difference from Communist equality.

The men fight over food, turning into little more than animals led by a cruel Nationalist leader. Yuan wonders at the men's quick deterioration. "When led by the Communists, they had been good soldiers and seemed high-minded and their lives had possessed a purpose, but now they were on the verge of becoming animals. How easily could humanity deteriorate in wretched conditions?"

Yuan begins to attend English religious services to practice his language skills. He asks Father Woodworth for a Bible in order to have something to read and translates some hymns into Chinese. The translations expose him as an English speaker to the camps' leaders, who try to convince him to sign up to go to Taiwan. The leaders begin a campaign of tattooing anti-Communist slogans on people's bodies to prove their loyalty to the Nationalist cause.

Commissar Pei is exposed and tortured, though he still refuses to admit that he is a Communist officer. Despite his leg not being properly healed, Yuan goes on a work-detail duty outside the camp. There he sees his friend Wanlin impaled on a fencepost. Though there are many opportunities to escape, no Chinese prisoners attempt to do so. The Korean prisoners, on the other hand, are much better organized and try to flee.

Yuan's Communist connection, Ming, informs him that Wanlin was executed because he had exposed Commissar Pei, a fact Yuan does not believe. Despite continued pressure to go to Taiwan, Yuan still refuses, saying that his duty is to his mother and his fiancée.

Yuan is attacked and wakes to find an anti-Communist slogan tattooed on his stomach in English. "The tattoo terrified me. With these words on me, how could I return to China?" The division and rivalries between the Nationalists and the Communists only deepen, turning increasingly threatening and violent. The

Nationalist leader cuts out a man's Communist tattoo with a knife, then murders him for expressing his desire to return to mainland China. The Nationalist leaders say everyone must leave their tattoo behind if they choose to go back to China. It is clear that death is in store for anyone who resists the Nationalists. The men decide that, "Above all, we had to survive." Yuan pledges to go to Taiwan, but the next day, he is brought to a tent where an American officer explains the Geneva Convention and the prisoners' right to return home. Yuan declares his intention to return to the mainland and is put in a camp for repatriation, or being returned to one's home country.

In the new camp, Commissar Pei is back in charge. Yuan shows him the tattoo, but Pei says not to worry for the moment. Yuan applies for membership in the United Communist Association. Yuan's Communist cohort Ming is also in the compound and tells Yuan that they might not accept his application because he translated hymns for Father Woodworth and often reads the Bible. Yuan despairs: "I had placed my fate with the Communists, but would they ever trust me? To them I had always been a marked man with a problematic past."

At his examination hearing, Yuan is accused of having an inappropriate relationship with Dr. Greene, but Ming saves him. Yuan is forced to give up his Bible. In the camp, he is in charge of translating the American newspaper *Stars and Stripes*, and he selectively imparts information, which gives him a sense of power. He befriends many of the American guards. One asks for a safety certificate, a letter in Chinese saying the American is a friend to the Chinese, so that if he gets captured, he may be treated more leniently.

On work duty one day, the leaders ask Yuan to steal a pistol from a sleeping soldier. Yuan does so to prove his loyalty. So he is invited to meet with the Korean prisoners' leaders. They reveal their plan to kidnap General Bell, the American commander of the prison camp. The plan is to invite him to speak to the Chinese, lull him into a sense of security, and then to seize him when he visits the Koreans.

The Chinese send Bell a letter with their demands for better treatment. When he does not respond, they begin a hunger strike. General Bell arrives at the compound, and Yuan translates their demands for better food. Yuan secretly believes the U.S. government treats them well, issuing plenty of clothing and bedrolls. Bell agrees to improve medical care and food, and the Chinese end the hunger strike.

Yuan is summoned by the Americans to a meeting. The Koreans have captured Bell. The next day, the prisoners voice their grievances in front of Bell, accusing his men of rape, cruelty, and torture. A Chinese man says he was nearly tricked into going to Taiwan. They accuse Bell of letting the Nationalists run the camps, of not taking control of the prisoners. Yuan loses his temper and yells at Bell; the general admits partial guilt for the circumstances. Bell issues a written statement, saying he will stop the violence in the camps. The Chinese and Koreans release him and celebrate their victory.

It is announced that everyone will be moved to Cheju Island. Yuan negotiates to have Commissar Pei accompany them on the boat trip, for which he receives accolades. Pei has become a revered figure among the prisoners, the embodiment of the Communist Party. The boat trip to Cheju is horrific. The men are stuffed into cabins where there is not enough room to sit down. Oil barrels serve as toilets, and they are soon overflowing.

The camp, though, is an improvement over the previous one. Commissar Pei is placed in jail on the island. Soon, Yuan is sent to jail after a guard finds a piece of paper in his pocket containing simply the lyrics to a song. Yuan is not upset, as he will finally be able to communicate with Pei. October 1 marks the Chinese National Day. The men make secret flags to fly and plot to kill some of the guards. There is a skirmish, and nearly 60 Chinese men are killed. A second revolt leads to more deaths. The Chinese prisoners retaliate with a hunger strike, which is resolved when the camp's captain agrees to investigate the deaths.

Four officers are chosen to go to Pusan to be "reregistered," which means interrogated. Pei's right-hand man, Ming, is chosen to go, but Pei insists that Yuan go in his place, taking his identification card. Yuan is angry; he believes that Pei has been manipulating him, and because Yuan is not a party member, he is expendable. He worries that if he leaves his comrades, he will later be falsely accused by the Communists of collaborating with the enemy. On the boat, Yuan considers dropping the fake identification tag he has been given in the water. It has Ming's fingerprints on it and could incriminate him; but Yuan is too afraid to do so.

The other men claim that the reregistration is routine, so Yuan destroys the fake card. When they question him, his fingerprints do not match those on file, Ming's, so they put him into solitary confinement. He debates telling the truth but fears that the Communists will accuse him of treason. The next day, the American officers say they know his true identity. Yuan admits that he was sent in place of Ming because he was not a Party member and therefore deemed nonessential. They ask if he is disgusted with the Communists, and he shows them his anti-Communist tattoo. They do not believe he is a Communist sympathizer, but he insists they call Chief Wang at the Nationalist camp to prove his story. Satisfied that he is telling the truth, they make it clear that they will not send him back to the Communist camp. Yuan has no choice but to agree to go to Taiwan.

Back at the pro-Nationalist camp, Yuan is happy to find Chief Wang still in charge. He is free to read there and studies the bilingual Bible he has been given. Among the prisoners, anti-Communist grievances are aired. Yuan understands that he has served as a tool of the Chinese government, and realizes why the Koreans do not like the Chinese, who consume Korean resources. "Whoever won this war," Yuan observes, "Korea would be a loser."

Conditions at the camp are better. The men grow vegetables and raise animals. There is more food, and they can come and go as they like; the guards are more lenient. Word arrives that an armistice has been signed at Panmunjom: The war is over. Before going to Taiwan, though, the men must undergo "persuasion." Though they are assured that the Americans will respect their wishes not to return to China, Yuan is disappointed, because he still harbors hope that he will be reunited with his mother and fiancée. Yuan worries about the repercussions to his family if he is identified as a Nationalist. He wants to return to China but does not know how.

Arriving at the "persuasion" tent, Yuan is happy to see an old friend from the Communist camp. He convinces Yuan that all is forgiven, and that the party will respect his sacrifice for Pei and not blame him for returning to the Nationalist camp. Yuan explains that he feels torn between the groups, but the friend convinces him to come back to China. He is reunited with Commissar Pei and Ming. They are happy to see him and invite him to join the Communist Party. Yuan says he will think about it.

Before returning to China, the prisoners must undergo "education," where they learn to be ashamed that they were held captive. Contrary to what they had been promised, everyone who was a leader in the camps is accused of betraying state secrets. Despite the courage Yuan displayed in the camps, he is still frequently interrogated. He receives a letter from Julan's older brother who says that his mother passed away a year ago and that if he really cares for Julan, he will never contact her again.

Yuan is devastated. If he had known that there was nothing to return to, he would not have tried so hard to return to his homeland. He mails Julan the jade barrette she gave him when he left for war but never hears from her. Yuan realizes that the Chinese government never planned to allow the prisoners to return. Even Commissar Pei was viewed as undesirable. "He, too, was war trash."

The following summer, the men are allowed to return to China. Because they had taken an oath that they would never let themselves be captured, they are dishonorably discharged, labeled as traitors or spies, and placed under surveillance. Yuan fares better than most who returned to their villages, becoming a teacher. He marries a fellow teacher and has two children, both of whom graduate from college. His son goes to the United States to get his master's degree and marries an American. Yuan has two American grandchildren. Visiting his son in the United States, Yuan decides to have his tattoo removed. An old comrade tells him that Commissar Pei's dying words were "Please write our story." Yuan fulfills the request yet warns the reader, "But do not take this to be an 'our story.' In the depths of my being I have never been one of them. I have just written what I experienced."

## Major Themes

### Alienation

This novel differs from others examined in this volume, as it does not take place in the United States and therefore does not deal specifically with the immigrant experience. Yet, in many ways, Yuan is as much an immigrant as many of the other characters featured in Asian-American fiction.

Separated from his homeland, his sense of place and belonging, Yuan grows increasingly alienated—from himself and from those around him. He complains constantly of his loneliness. He feels cast out of society, able to fit in neither with the Communists nor the Nationalists, neither the Americans nor the Koreans. This is partly his own doing; he deliberately separates himself from the men, spending time alone.

Another factor that separates Yuan from his fellow prisoners is his education. Both political parties view educated men with suspicion. His knowledge of English makes him useful to his superiors but also further sets him apart from the other men. He is viewed by many as necessary but not to be trusted. He likes to read, a solitary occupation, and his only source of literature is the Bible, which continues to make others even more suspicious of him.

Yuan's intelligence and insight into his situation alienate him further. He is able to see both sides of an argument and is not swayed by either party's propaganda. He can detect hypocrisy and deception in the behavior of both the Nationalists and Communists. On the one hand, he respects the Communists for restoring order to China. On the other, he hates their method of forcing Communist beliefs and teachings on the people. He approves of socialism and equality but eventually realizes that the Communist leaders are as corrupt as the Nationalists. Most of all, he feels frustrated at his role as a pawn in someone else's game, a game that he cannot win. He can only survive.

Throughout the novel, he is able to focus on the beauty of his surroundings, the sound of women singing, the stunning mountains, the views of the ocean. He continuously reminds himself that there are others worse off than he is. When he discovers that all attempts to return to China to fulfill his duty to his mother and honor his promise to Julan are futile, he accepts the cruel irony with stoicism. His alienation has helped him separate himself, as much as possible, from the horrors and bitter realities of war.

## Human Cruelty and Brutality

Another observation that Jin asserts through the trials of his protagonist is that humankind can be cruel and brutish. The men—bored, scared, and hungry—fight over food or what little status or power that can achieved in the camps. Yuan's philosophy that there must be some higher meaning to life, a supreme being who "multiplies" one's actions and elevates them to a level of importance, is of little solace. He realizes that this is a form of idealism, the same way that Pei's attachment to Communism is a sort of religion.

Other conclusions that Yuan draws about the men around him is that they are social beings. "Singing was a cathartic experience for the prisoners." Singing together lessened their loneliness, "enabled them to identify with one another emotionally so as to increase their feeling of solidarity." Of course, Yuan leaves himself out of the scenario; he is able to observe but not participate.

Yuan can also be critical if not cruel in the opinions he holds and generalizations he makes about the Chinese character. Throughout, he compares Chinese to Koreans and Americans. He explains that someone is "gregarious, as most Chinese are." The Chinese do not try to escape: "Like any ordinary Chinese, I was also afflicted with timidity." He marvels at the differences between the various cultures brought together by the war. One American GI admires his leader for athleticism: "General Bell is a good man. He played baseball with us. He's a powerful pitcher." Yuan wonders "What did Bell's character have to do with sports?"

### Bearing Witness

Yuan states that this is the first and last time he will write. In addition, he is writing in English, his second language. Though the grammar is perfect, Yuan's re-creation of the dialogue is often stiff and stilted and suggests he is translating from his native tongue. Characters say things such as, "Come on, stop trying to hoodwink this old man." Such elements remind the reader that this is the story that played out in a foreign land and in a foreign language, which only increases the sense of distance and alienation that is so key to the novel.

Yuan writes his narrative in a detached manner, rarely letting the reader feel or experience his emotions, describing his moods and mental state directly and bluntly instead: "I was angry." This serves to further distance the reader from the narrative, so that Yuan's purpose, to tell the tale but not admit it is his own, is achieved. Yuan is only writing to record the history. "Who can bear the weight of a war?" he asks. "To witness is to make the truth known, but we must remember that most victims have no voice of their own, and that in bearing witness to their stories we must not appropriate them." In telling the tale of Chinese prisoners in Korea, Jin's protagonist Yuan is able to view his own history from an outsider's perspective.

## *Waiting*
### Summary and Analysis

With the line, "Every summer Lin Kong returned to Goose Village to divorce his wife, Shuyu," the waiting that gives this novel its title begins. The story of a doctor in love with a woman who is not his wife, *Waiting* explores modern Chinese society and the endurance of love.

It is 1983. Lin Kong lives in Muji City, where he works as a doctor in a military hospital. Separated from his wife for twenty years by Communist Party demands, he has been celibate for 17. His girlfriend at the hospital, Manna Wu, insists that he try to obtain a divorce, but every year when Lin goes back to his village for his twelve-day leave, his wife initially agrees and then refuses to divorce him once they reach the court.

At home, Lin notices how foreign the village seems, how stuck in time it appears to be. His daughter, a teenager named Hua, seems like a country bumpkin he hardly knows. Once again, Lin and his wife make their annual trip to divorce court. Shuyu's brother Bensheng accompanies them; Lin is sure it is he who encourages Shuyu to stay married. Yet again, Bensheng speaks up for Shuyu, saying that she wants to stay married. Lin is filled with shame when the judge rebukes him for using his wife and leaving her like "a donkey at the millstone." The judge reminds him that he is a revolutionary officer who should be "a model for us civilians." When Lin returns to Manna, she is unemotional; this is a familiar disappointment.

Manna Wu has been waiting for Lin to get divorced for 17 years. According to army rules, couples could only get a contested divorce after 18 years of separation. Meanwhile, Manna and Lin have been in a chaste relationship for 17 years. Both have roommates since they are unmarried, and hospital rules prevent them from being together in any way outside the hospital compound.

The novel then traces the history of their relationship. The recently heartbroken student Manna delivers a journal to Lin in his room and sees that he has more than 200 books, including some foreign and subversive titles that would certainly be banned by party leaders. She begins to borrow his books, more out of curiosity about him than about the books themselves. She learns that other officers, who should be reporting Lin's disobedience to party leaders, are instead borrowing books themselves. Lin asks her to come over to help him cover his books so that the titles do not show. They work quietly, aware of their attraction, which deepens over time. Manna soon becomes obsessed with Lin, dropping by to visit him and thinking about him constantly. She knows he is married but cannot control or alter her feelings. When she sees him walking with another nurse, she is wracked with jealousy.

Lin becomes aware of Manna's attentions, and though he feels sorry for her because she is an orphan, he is not ready to return the affection. He is frustrated that he lives so far from his wife and daughter. He feels gratitude to his wife for caring for his elderly parents, but no love. He resents Manna for disturbing his tranquil life. One day she leaves an envelope containing an opera ticket on his desk. When he goes to the theater, she is sitting in the seat next to him. When the lights go down, she takes his hand and caresses it. Lin is terrified by the show of affection and quickly leaves. When he sees her the next day he is embarrassed, but she acts as if nothing had happened.

They arrange to meet later in the week. He decides that if "this leads to an affair, so be it." Still, they grow worried about how their close friendship appears to others in the compound. They begin to meet more often and are soon inseparable. Lin reminds himself that he is a married man. Everyone is gossiping about them, though the couple displays no signs of having been intimate.

Lin is summoned to see Ran Su, the vice-director of the hospital's political department and a friend. Ran Su warns Lin that people are talking about him. His relationship with Manna may affect his future. Lin promises that the relationship will remain platonic. He wishes he could go back to the time when he did not yet know Manna.

He tells her about the meeting, and she demands to know how he feels about her. He tells her he loves her, but they must stay merely friends or face punishment from the establishment. "I'd be a happy man if she were my wife, he thought." As if to prove his suspicions true, Lin is not given the distinction of being elected as a model officer that year. His relationship is indeed causing political and career problems.

Manna becomes obsessed with knowing what Lin's wife, Shuyu, looks like. She is surprised when she sees Shuyu's photograph. She looks and dresses like an old woman. Manna laughs at her bound feet, an old-fashioned practice. Angry, Lin storms off.

Manna arranges for them to be alone, but Lin feels it is too risky. He wonders if he will be able to control his desire in her presence. Lin's father dies. Shuyu does not have to care for his parents anymore; he feels free. He could divorce her and have "a marriage based on love and a wife whose appearance wouldn't embarrass him." But he also feels guilty for trying to discard his wife after she has served his family so admirably.

Manna demands that he divorce his wife. She then stops speaking to him. Drunk at the National Day Party, sobbing and apologizing, she follows Lin outside. He takes her home, puts her in her bed, and leaves, beginning to think seriously about divorcing Shuyu.

Back home that summer, Lin finds himself growing attached to his daughter and she to him. He finds he likes the once unpleasant country setting. The couple gets along well. Lin even wonders if he had stayed in the countryside, might he have learned to love Shuyu? When she asks for another child, he refuses. Lin is suddenly aware of the nature of Shuyu's plight. She believes they will be together forever and feels lonely. She works like a servant, denying herself food and clothing in order to save his money. Lin feels increasingly guilty. He wishes he could have two wives. Returning to the hospital, Lin urges Manna to seek a husband. She cries, saying she cannot get a transfer and that everyone in the hospital already views her as his wife.

The following year, Lin returns to the village with a letter from Ran Su recommending his divorce. Manna is hopeful, but Lin returns with the news that Bensheng "went berserk . . . turned the whole village against him." Lin's brother-in-law even threatened to come to the hospital to expose the couple, and Lin becomes worried that Ran Su could be implicated as well. Lin says they should not cause trouble before the next round of promotions, when he and Manna each receive a higher rank and a raise in salary. "The promotion pleased them, although it had cost them much more than it had other people."

Part 2 begins in 1972. Lin's cousin Liang Meng is a widower who is looking to remarry, but, after meeting, he and Manna prove a poor match. The following year at the divorce court yields the same results. The judge demands to know Manna's name, which Lin is too afraid to reveal. The judge takes this to be an admission that Lin has had an affair and so dismisses the case.

At the hospital, Commissar Wei appears, recently divorced and looking for a fiancée, specifically a nurse to take care of him in his old age. Ren Su asks if Lin is opposed to introducing Manna to him. Lin has conflicted feelings, reluctantly saying that it might be good for her. He is relieved at the prospect of not having to try to divorce his wife every year. Wei invites Manna to a movie. They talk of books, and he asks her to read *Leaves of Grass* and let him know what she thinks of the often sensual nineteenth-century American poems. Afraid she will expose her lack of education or insight, Manna has Lin write the assessment. When she copies the report and gives it to Wei, he finds her handwriting too sloppy or perhaps he is disappointed at the strict Communist interpretation. Uninterested in Manna as a result, he marries a younger woman instead. Manna is humiliated and makes Lin promise he will not make her try to find another man.

Lin contracts tuberculosis. In the hospital, he shares a room with Commissar Wei's associate Geng Yang, who assumes that Manna is Lin's fiancée. Lin tells him the reality of the situation. Though he is shocked by Geng Yang's crude and often unrestrained manner of speaking, the two grow close. Lin eventually tells him the story of his attempts to divorce Shuyu.

Geng Yang suggests that Lin stop trying to divorce Shuyu and simply keep Manna as a mistress. "You can't be nice to everybody can you? In this case, damage is unavoidable. You have to choose which one of them to hurt." Lin knows that Geng Yang is right and worries that he has been using Manna.

Lin leaves for a course in another city. Geng Yang asks Manna to come by his room to pick up two of Lin's books. Manna admires his assertiveness and wishes Lin was more like Geng Yang. In his room, she discovers him in his pajamas, drunk. He grabs her and tells her he knows she is interested in him, that she likes him more than that "sissy" Lin who will not commit to her. Though she struggles, he overpowers her, raping her while she curses his family.

Ashamed, Manna assumes Geng Yang will call to apologize, but he never does. She is relieved to discover she is not pregnant. Lin returns to find her changed, older looking. When she tells him what happened, Lin does not respond. Manna grows angry, remembering that Lin told Geng Yang that she was a virgin. Lin's unwillingness to speak troubles her. "What if your own man doesn't believe you?" Meanwhile, Manna's friend Haiyan has spread news of the rape. Manna is furious with her. It becomes clear to Manna that she now has no choice but to wait for Lin "as though the two of them had been predestined to be inseparable."

The narrative then jumps ahead several years. Manna and Lin, unlike their colleagues, never get promotions. Ran Su becomes director of the hospital, and

Commissar Wei dies in prison. In 1984, Lin summons Shuyu to the hospital, determined to divorce her after the requisite 18 years' separation.

Part 3 brings the narrative into the present. Shuyu comes to Muji City, a spectacle because of her bound feet, yet everyone likes her and begins to feel sorry for her because they know that Lin is planning to divorce her. Lin gets Shuyu and Hua's residency permits changed to the city, though Hua wishes to remain in the country. Shuyu gets her hair cut in a modern bob, which makes her look years younger. The hairdresser tells her to climb into Lin's bed, and Shuyu replies, "I won't do that," which becomes a ridiculed and much-repeated catchphrase around the hospital. Lin and Shuyu's problems are everyone's joke, but the divorce, after so many years, goes smoothly. It is all over in half an hour. Manna and Lin plan to get married in a few months, after the gossip has died down.

Lin goes to Goose Village to sell his house and try to convince Hua to come to the city with him. A drunken Bensheng seems to be genuinely upset that Hua is leaving—he and his wife consider Hua to be their own daughter. He passes out, and Lin has to carry him home. He is surprised that Bensheng is capable of real feeling. "The load on his back grew heavier and heavier."

Hua and Shuyu move to an apartment, and Lin and Manna finally get married. The wedding, after so many years, is anticlimactic. After the ceremony, Manna, sick with a cold, is taken home. Custom demands that Lin stay at the chaotic wedding and be the host, but he cannot prevent himself from thinking "how bored he was by their wedding." Manna's passion proves overwhelming for the newlywed Lin. She becomes pregnant and insists they sleep in separate beds so as not to harm the baby. Hua visits and says that her mother is glad to hear about the pregnancy—it means their family will increase. Lin finds this point of view strange. He finds love letters from the boyfriend Manna dated as a young woman and is amazed at the intensity of his feeling. Lin has never felt passionate about anyone.

He looks back with fondness on the serenity of his life before he married Manna. He finds marriage exhausting. When he starts tutoring female orderlies, jealously and distance creep into the marriage. A grumpy Manna goes into early labor. During the painful birth, she calls Lin names and curses him, accusing him of being a "miser" for his inability to pay off Bensheng years ago. Called back to the labor room by the sound of cries, Lin sees that Manna has given birth to twin boys. Their shrunken, wrinkled skin is repulsive to him, and watching Haiyan sew up Manna's tear produces a wave of nausea. He carries the boys home and imagines that he might trade places with them, starting his life anew.

Manna is not making a strong recovery. A cardiogram reveals a heart condition. She cannot walk, so Lin must pace the floor with the crying babies at night. When the twins fall ill with dysentery, Lin realizes how much he loves his two sons. When they grow weaker, Hua arrives. Shuyu has suggested giving the twins mashed taro root, white sugar, and egg yolk to restore their health. The folk remedy proves rapidly successful.

Manna's condition continues to deteriorate, and Lin takes over most of the household duties, including laundry, which Shuyu and Manna had always done for him. Manna eventually returns to work part time, but her manner has grown nagging and childish. When Lin burns rice one day, she throws a tantrum. "I hate her!" Lin thinks. He wonders if he ever really loved the woman he waited so long to marry. He feels he has been "a sleepwalker, pulled and pushed about by others' opinions, by external pressure by . . . illusions, by the official rules." Though the couple makes up, Lin has lingering fantasies of running away.

One evening, bringing food to Hua and Shuyu, Lin sees them through the window, the perfect portrait of domesticity. They invite him into the warm room, give him some liquor, and Lin grows maudlin, realizing that the two women are doing fine without him. He wishes he could have a peaceful life, not the unstable marriage he is stuck in. Lin begs Shuyu to forgive him, calling her sweetheart. He feels he has made a terrible mistake and begs Shuyu to wait for him, assuring her that Manna will die soon and that then he will return to her. He passes out at Shuyu's house.

When he returns home the next morning, he finds an equally tranquil scene. Hua arrives for a visit, the babies are cooing and content, and Manna is loving. Hua reminds him of his alcohol-fueled promise from the night before. Lin tells his daughter to inform Shuyu that he was drunk and did not mean it, that she should not wait for him. "We'll always wait for you," Hua says. Lin feels the burden of his responsibilities increase. He has trapped himself again. When Manna wishes a passerby "Happy Spring Festival," he notices that her voice sounds hearty, "still resonant with life."

## Major Themes

### The Inability to Act

Unsurprisingly, given the title, the novel's central theme revolves around notions of waiting. Delayed gratification is examined from all points of view in the work. Lin, as the protagonist, is the primary victim. He delays all personal satisfaction until he can divorce his wife and marry Manna. As such, he spends nearly twenty years in suspended animation. He does not live at all, instead looking ahead to a vague and undefined future. His inability to act affects nearly everyone around him.

Always quick to blame other people or his situation for his misfortunes, Lin is essentially a passive character who lets his life slip by. He feels constantly constrained by duty, first to his parents, at whose request he marries Shuyu, then to his obligation to Shuyu, his duties to the state and its rules, and then, finally, to Manna. Not once does he examine what he truly wants and then pursue and achieve it. Instead, he is trapped, stuck in his inability to act or seize control. Many times there are opportunities to insist on a divorce from Shuyu. Instead Lin falls victim to his own guilt and never makes a serious or sustained effort at securing his freedom. Part of his indecisiveness and stasis stems from his kindness. He does not want to hurt the women in his life. Nonetheless, through his inaction, he ends up injuring them both.

## Human Passivity and Constraint

Shuyu waits as well. She is a throwback to a different era, with her bound feet and her undying devotion to her husband, even though he has essentially abandoned her. She relishes her self-sacrifice, saving money and denying herself pleasures and necessities, all in service to her absent husband. She is presented as a simple character, unable to think ill of her husband, sad only that she is unable to please him.

Of the three main characters, Manna is the least passive, though she is so constrained by society that she has little choice but to wait for Lin. As a young woman, she attempts to marry for love but is jilted by her practical fiancé who does not want to endure hardship for her. Though she later attempts several times to end her "affair" with Lin, the couple always comes back together. She meets Lin's cousin and dates Commissar Wei, but her experiences with these men are so negative that she decides she is better off waiting for Lin than attempting to find another partner. Still, she is never able to do anything more than beg Lin to divorce. She does not lend him the money to pay off Bensheng, and she continues to treat him as her husband, spending all her time with him and doing his laundry. She halfheartedly searches for a way out of the romantic connection but is ultimately content when her attempts fail.

The narrative style mimics this waiting as well. Ha Jin chooses to start the story the year before the divorce. By doing so, the reader knows in advance the outcome of the various trips to Goose Village. Jin has removed any thread of suspense from his plot. So, by extension, the reader is waiting, as well. When the divorce and marriage finally occur, they are anticlimactic, containing no sense of joy or triumph, after so many years of obstacles. The narrative style mimics Lin's detachment as well, narrating the events and the thoughts of the characters with an unemotional remove and a lack of critical judgment.

## Government Control of Individual Lives

Part of what constrains the characters is the Communist state, full of obscure rules and strict control. Jin uses the story of Lin and Manna to criticize the hypocrisy and absurdity of Communist China. The rule that couples are not to appear together outside the hospital grounds has endured from former times. The man who enforced the rule is long dead, yet the restriction remains in place out of habit. All the characters fear what the government will do to them if they dare disobey. For

Lin, expulsion from the military means poverty and a posting in a remote place. He would also lose whatever small privilege he is afforded as a professional. The Communist-influenced government and policies, which were meant to eliminate class, have merely created a different form of aristocracy, with a small group of individuals wielding great power over the masses.

In the novel, the government is exposed as ridiculous. When Lin is criticized for his relationship with Manna, he is able to deflect the unwanted attention by merely cutting his hair to look more like other party members. The officers demand that people turn in "subversive" books but continue to borrow them from Lin and look the other way. The 400-mile forced march Manna endures while a trainee is an exercise in absurdity that serves no purpose but to injure the hospital staff. Still, Manna and Lin abide by the rules. Lin searches for Maoist and Communist teachings in Walt Whitman's poetry, unable to approach or appreciate the writing in any other light. It never occurs to him that Commissar Wei might be looking for a wife who is an independent thinker. By turning in a report that panders to the Communist Party line, Lin and Manna potentially destroy her chance for happiness.

In contrast to Lin and Manna, those who break the rules in the novel seem to be better off than those who conform to them. Commissar Wei is obviously somewhat of a rebel, reading forbidden Western poetry, a man who does not believe in strict party politics. Additionally Geng Yang, a rapist and an immoral man, gets rich by capitalizing on the new Chinese economic opportunities. He leaves the army and becomes successful, proving that it is possible for Manna and Lin to find a new life outside their chosen careers.

### The Role of Women

Those who have the least opportunity for choice, however, are the women in the book. Shuyu is trapped in her loveless marriage. If Lin leaves her, she will be unable to feed herself. Her parents bound her feet to make her more attractive, yet they make Lin embarrassed to be seen with her. She is so hobbled and in such pain from the foot binding that she is unable to draw water. Manna, too, is inhibited by her status as a woman. She is unable to find a boyfriend because the unmarried officers look for potential partners in town, where they can avoid being reprimanded for their actions. Once she has been labeled "Lin's girlfriend," she cannot get anyone else to pay attention to her. At the age of 28, her prospects have begun to dwindle. She has little opportunity to determine or influence her own destiny. She neglects to report her rape because she fears that no one will believe her. Geng Yang finds the fact that Manna is a virgin amusing rather than a status to be respected and preserved.

### A Changing Society

The "New China," though more liberal than previous regimes, is nonetheless stuck in the past. Each visit Lin pays to Goose Village reminds him of the gap that exists between modern city life and ancient rural life. In Goose Village, any attempt at an intellectual life is pointless. His books are not valued and only grow mold. The society functions according to a feudal system, where women are considered property, and displeasure at modern mores (such as divorce) prompts the villagers to form a mob. In this light, modern Manna, who is able to give birth at 44, is a sharp contrast to Shuyu, with her bound feet.

## The Changing Nature of Desire

Lin is so divorced from his emotions and from a sense of what he wants that the fulfillment of his long-held goals is no longer what he wishes. The obstacle to marrying Manna seems to be what he is most interested in. Once that obstacle is removed, he is bored by his wedding, shocked at Manna's physical passion, and longs for what he once most ardently wanted to escape—his life with Shuyu. Mostly, he wants no one to make demands on him and then feels sorry for himself for never having felt the passion of true love. This pattern plays out again and again in the novel, most notably in the final pages when Lin is unhappy to have two sons, a sign of luck in China. He wants to return to Shuyu's house, asking her to wait for him much as he did with Manna, and then changes his mind, even though he has already made a promise. With Manna returned to health, she will most likely live for many years. Lin's remarriage to Shuyu is thus delayed, starting the cycle over once again. The characters know no other life but one dominated by their need to wait and endure.

Jin seems to be emphasizing the notion that life occurs and is experienced while we are waiting for it to begin. By focusing on a distant goal, Lin lets his life slip away. He constantly questions his motivations and true feelings, but in truth he is never able to break from his own sense of duty or his own restrictive situation. He is unable to fully act, to seize control, or to come to a conclusion. He deludes himself into thinking his restraint can be traced to the fact that he is an intellectual and a rational scientist. He believes he is the only one caught in a struggle between reason and emotion. In his self-absorption, he is surprised and embarrassed to find that others are too. In the end, only Hua, a simple young woman with no education, is able to love freely and completely. Excessively thinking about the best course of action, overanalyzing, Jin suggests, stifles and replaces emotion, much less the ability to act. By risking nothing, the characters gain nothing.

# CHANG-RAE LEE

## Biography

CHANG-RAE LEE WAS born in South Korea on July 29, 1965. When he was three years old, his family moved to the suburbs of New York, where his father practiced psychiatry. Lee attended boarding school and graduated from Yale University. He received his M.F.A. in creative writing from the University of Oregon and spent a year as a Wall Street financial analyst before turning to fiction writing as a full-time profession.

Throughout his career, Lee has taught creative writing at Princeton University, Hunter College, and other institutions. He lives outside New York City with his wife, an architect, and their two young daughters and is an avid golfer in his spare time. His debut novel, *Native Speaker*, published in 1995, was an immediate success, winning the PEN/Hemingway Award, the American Book Award, the Barnes and Noble Discover Award and named an American Library Association Notable Book of the Year.

Continuing to explore the theme of alienation, particularly as it relates to the Asian-American male, Lee's second novel, *A Gesture Life*, examines the effects of World War II on a Korean immigrant in the United States. "I'm fascinated by people who find themselves in positions of alienation or some kind of cultural dissonance," he has said. "The characters may not always be Asian Americans, but they will always be people who are thinking about the culture and how they fit or don't fit into it." *A Gesture Life* continued to win Lee accolades, including the Anisfield-Wolf Literary Award, the Gustavus Myers Outstanding Book Award, and the NAIBA (North Atlantic Independent Booksellers Association) Book Award for Fiction. The novel was also cited as a Notable Book of Year by the *New York Times, Esquire, Publishers Weekly,* and the *Los Angeles Times.* Lee's third novel, *Aloft* (2004), fits his pattern and central interests; its Italian-American protagonist is struggling to find his identity in America's melting pot. His fourth novel, *The Surrendered,* was published in 2010.

Lee himself does not share his protagonists' feelings of separation and anxiety. He calls his craft a "regular job," and though he laments that "being a Korean-American novelist doesn't quite include being an American novelist," he has found his place on the shelves of readers of all backgrounds, allowing them a glimpse into the complicated world of the immigrant.

## *Native Speaker*
### Summary and Analysis

*Native Speaker* opens as its first-person narrator, Henry Park, reveals that his "American" wife has left him, giving him a long list of his faults as a husband before leaving. They met at a party, where she impressed him with her understanding of his unique situation: born in Korea, raised in the United States. "You look like someone listening to himself," she noted.

In his newly single life, other mysteries begin to unfold. Henry works as a corporate spy, befriending other immigrants and reporting trade secrets and business intrigue back to his boss, Dennis Hoagland. His co-workers are also immigrants, from various corners of the globe, including his friend Jack Kalantzakos, an expert in Mediterranean affairs. Jack's wife died of cancer, and the two men bond over their shared loss. Jack was also a friend to Henry's son, Mitt, who is mentioned only in flashback.

Henry is asked to research John Kwang, the "prince of Northern Boulevard," an up-and-coming Korean-American politician. The task is supposed to be easy, a second chance after a failed attempt to ingratiate himself as a patient of Dr. Emile Luzan, a Filipino psychoanalyst. Dr. Luzan was organizing a movement to return Ferdinand Marcos to power, and Henry was sent in to find out anything he could about the doctor. When the therapy sessions got too personal, Hoagland called them off, and Henry, breaking protocol to telephone to apologize for the abrupt end to his sessions, was shocked to find out that Dr. Luzan had died in a boating accident.

Kwang is married with two children, a pillar of the Queens immigrant community in New York City. Henry is to pose as a volunteer on Kwang's campaign for city council. Hoagland tells Henry, "Just stay in the background. Be unapparent and flat. . . . This thing with Kwang should be quick and clean." Mostly, Hoagland wants to know the origins of Kwang's money. He relies on small contributions from local small businesses like the ones Henry's father owned before his strokes. Perhaps, Henry thinks, Kwang has profited from a *ggeh*, a money club popular among Korean Americans, where each contributes a small amount of money and the participants then take turns using the capital.

Henry's father owned a small grocery store/deli until Henry's mother died when he was a boy, after which his father threw himself into his work, adding two more stores to his small empire. He treats his employees and customers with contempt. Though he was an educated man in South Korea, his lack of English prevented him from finding a white-collar job in the United States. He insisted on Henry's education, hoping for better opportunities for his son. The two lived together in near silence until, one day, Henry's father went to the airport and came home with a Korean woman who was to be their servant. Though she lived with them for many years, Henry never knew her name and referred to her remotely as Ahjuhma, or "aunt," a form of polite address.

Henry's wife, Leila, a frustrated poet and elementary school speech therapist, always found the situation appalling. During one summer that Henry, Leila, and Mitt spent at his father's house, escaping Manhattan for a visit, Leila insisted on engaging Ahjuhma in conversation, but the woman refused, not allowing Leila to perform any domestic tasks and eventually yelling at her in Korean, forcing Henry to tell Ahjuhma that she could not speak that way to his father's wife if she wished to continue to live in the house. Henry suspected, even hoped, that Ahjuhma and his father's relationship was deeper than master and servant.

At first, Henry's duties in Kwang's office are routine. When Henry diffuses a situation with a group of unhappy Peruvian immigrants, Kwang notices him. Henry begins to work with Kwang's closest advisors: Sherrie, his media manager; Janice, his scheduler; and Eduardo, a beefy college student and bodyguard. Together, they plot photo opportunities and lay out Kwang's days.

Henry is good at his job, both as a campaign worker and as a spy. "He couldn't offend anybody. So he looks friendly, he looks like he'd be willing to talk to you, but really because of the way his gaze circles about you, gets at your outline instead of your live center, you think he's really stepping back as he approaches, stepping back inside and back away from you so nothing can get around or behind him." He exploits and plays up the stereotype of the unthreatening Asian-American male to hide in the shadows and collect information.

Henry finally reveals that his son, Mitt, died on his seventh birthday. Having overcome the racial prejudice that plagued the suburbs, Mitt had a number of local friends at Henry's father's house. Henry was returning from buying party supplies when he saw everyone huddled around a limp form. Mitt had been smothered while the boys played dogpile, jumping on him and tackling him.

Leila has returned to New York City but is staying with her friend, Molly, who reports back to Henry on his ex-wife's activities. Henry asks to borrow some cassette tapes that Mitt recorded; they make him think of his wife. With a plan to discuss their future, Henry goes to Molly's house in the middle of the night, where he and Leila finally talk. She reveals that she had an affair after she left him and then berates him for never talking about their son: "You haven't said his name more than four or five times since it happened." When he says it was a terrible accident, she grows angry. "When your baby dies it's never an accident. . . . Sometimes I think it's more like some long-turning karma that finally came back for us. Or that we didn't love each other. We thought our life was good enough." Then Leila raises a racially based issue. "Maybe it's that Mitt wasn't all white or all yellow. . . . Maybe the world wasn't ready for him."

As Henry gets to know Kwang, he becomes impressed, even seduced by him.

> Before I knew of him, I had never even conceived of someone like him. A Korean man, of his age, as part of the vernacular. Not just a respectable grocer or dry cleaner or doctor, but a larger public figure who was willing to speak and act outside the tight sphere of his family. He displayed an ambition I didn't recognize, or more, one I hadn't yet envisioned as something a Korean man would find significant or worthy of energy and devotion."

Henry spins for himself a story of a Korean Great Gatsby, one who dresses well and transcends racial stereotypes. He describes Kwang as "my necessary invention." He sees in Kwang the same knowing intimacy he found with Dr. Luzan, who understood "the larger [issue] of where we live, my friend, and who you are within that place. Or believe yourself to be. We have our multiple roles like everyone else. Now throw in an additional dimension. A cultural one. Cast it all, if you will, in a broad yellow light." In other words, they are Asian-American men, struggling to find a place for themselves in a country that would potentially choose to render them invisible.

Politics turns serious when the African-American candidate for mayor is revealed to have been having an affair. A Korean man shoots an African-American woman, setting off tension in Queens. Then, at a speech, a young boy shoots at Kwang. Henry, genuinely alarmed, goes to speak to Jack, wondering if Jack knows something about Kwang that he has not revealed. Jack refuses to answer him, suggesting that he do his job and get out. Henry has already decided that this will be his last job for Hoagland.

Meanwhile, Henry and Kwang grow closer. Henry keeps a database of everyone who has contact with Kwang, and the politician takes the printouts home to memorize. One evening, he invites Henry to dinner. They talk as they drive through the neighborhood. Kwang made his money in selling dry-cleaning equipment. He is clearly a part of the community, diffusing a potentially serious disagreement between an African-American customer and a Korean store owner. Henry and Kwang eat Korean food and drink *soju* (a rice liquor), their bond growing all the more. Kwang speaks of the difficulty of being a politician and contemplates the secret to diplomacy. Speak "very softly," Henry says, "and to yourself."

Seduced by the liquor and Kwang's confidences, Henry feels himself abandoning the role of spy. Forgetting his training, he neglects to keep his wits about him. Luckily, the pair is interrupted by Sherrie, the media coordinator, who alludes to a serious situation. Henry then sees Kwang, a married man, touch Sherrie intimately on her back. His admiration for the politician starts to fade.

Henry admits as much to Leila when she joins him in cleaning out his father's house. They have been periodically seeing each other, re-establishing trust, and staying in the house together gives them a renewed intimacy. They move back in together in Manhattan. One evening, they watch a television news report of a two-alarm fire at the offices of Councilman John Kwang. A suspicious small explosion caused the fire. Kwang is safe, but Eduardo the college student and another worker were killed. Henry suspects Hoagland.

Henry is asked to deliver an envelope containing money to Eduardo's family. As he leaves, the woman thanks Henry, believing him to be Mr. Kwang. Henry goes to Kwang's house where Kwang informs him he will not try to discover who set the blaze; it does not matter to him. He asks Henry to take over Eduardo's secret job of cataloging illegal campaign contributions. Kwang is running a type of *ggeh*, doling out money to those who have contributed.

Henry reports these activities to Hoagland, but it appears as though Kwang is hiding something even more significant. Jack tells Henry that government investigators came to see Hoagland, and an illegal *ggeh* would not concern federal agents. Eduardo, it is revealed, had been renting an expensive Manhattan apartment, thereby raising suspicion. Rumors soon hit the press that Kwang is running "a pyramidal laundering scheme, a people's lottery, an Asian numbers game."

Kwang starts to unravel before Henry's eyes. Henry drives him to an after-hours club with Sherrie, where Kwang gets violent with a waitress. He tells Henry that Eduardo was not stealing from him, nor was Kwang giving Eduardo money. Instead, Eduardo betrayed his boss. During these confessions, Henry finally realizes that, like him, Eduardo was also working for Hoagland.

The next morning, Henry awakens to the news that Kwang has been arrested. He was in a car accident with the waitress from the restaurant, who is only sixteen and in critical condition. Kwang posts bail and disappears. With the money club being reported in the news, officers representing Immigration and Naturalization Services have taken the money club list and arrested everyone on it who is an illegal immigrant. Protestors stand outside Kwang's house, demanding to see him and asking him to resign.

Henry contemplates the differences between Kwang and his father. Henry's dead mother would have accused Kwang of reaching too high, of being too ambitious, and Henry sees how his father had to "retool his life to the ambitions his meager knowledge of the language and culture would allow, invent again the man he wanted to be." Even with this understanding, Henry confesses that he still holds "troubling awe and contempt and piety . . . for his life."

Kwang goes to jail, and Henry quits his job to help Leila in her role as speech therapist. He dresses up as the "Speech Monster," pretending to be tamed by the correct pronunciation of the day's phrase. New York, he observes, is the "city of words . . . the constant cry is that you belong here, or you make yourself belong, or you must go." At the end, New York's diverse, multicultural culture pleases Henry. As Leila reads each student's name, "I hear her speaking a dozen lovely and native languages, calling all the difficult names of who we are."

# Major Themes

## Asian-American Male Stereotypes

Chang-rae Lee takes as one of his major themes the complicated situation of interracial marriage and the children such unions produce. He simultaneously presents and transforms the stereotype of the Asian man as passive and unable to attract women. Henry is far from submissive, until the death of his son leaves him awash in grief. He has no conflicts with his wife as long as it is just the two of them. His relationship with Leila becomes strained only when she tries to infiltrate the complicated mores and traditions of his strict Korean family.

That the outside world is not as accepting of racial difference is revealed, however, when Henry recalls how he was teated by his peers when he was younger. Mitt experiences the same racial slurs in suburban New York, showing how little things have changed since Henry's childhood. Henry wonders if perhaps the world is not ready for a biracial child. To seemingly confirm the unpleasant notion, Mitt is symbolically smothered in the novel, snuffed out by the rough-housing neighborhood boys.

Leila is unable to understand the constant care with which Henry must do everything—he has the weight of representing his entire culture on his shoulders. This is perhaps what draws him to Kwang and vice versa; they are both attempting to transcend the expectations society has set for them, without betraying or turning their backs on their culture. Kwang falls victim to exactly what Henry fears. In treading the thin line of assimilation and resistance, Kwang is pulled in many different directions and collapses under the impossibility of sustaining these multiple identities and burdens.

## The Father-Son Relationship

Kwang acts as Henry's surrogate father in the novel. Motherless, Henry has only his father, who is unable to be the American father Henry wishes. He mistreats his employees and yells at customers. He is racist and intolerant, and his relationship with Ahjuhma borders on exploitation. Henry searches, then, for surrogate or alternate father figures, in Jack at his office and in the psychologist Dr. Emile Luzan. That he later betrays Emile is a major source of guilt throughout the novel.

Similarly, the novel examines relationships between fathers and sons. In a more tragic repetition of how his father failed him, Henry does not save his son from the weight of the neighborhood's children, who pile on him and crush him in a symbolic and literally extreme form of racism. This sense of having failed to protect those he loves leads Henry to resist reporting Kwang to officials. By not alerting the law, Henry perhaps does Kwang more harm than confronting him or attempting to prevent his eventual breakdown and fall from grace.

## Language and Literary Allusion

The revelation of Kwang's flaws is a major disappointment to Henry, giving rise to a comparison to F. Scott Fitzgerald's *The Great Gatsby*, the classic American novel. As outsiders, both Lee's Henry and Fitzgerald's Nick admire the effortless rise and acceptance of the self-made important man. Their wealth is a source of envy, as is their ability to attract other people. Gatsby's domain is the affluent suburb of East Egg, while Kwang's is the culturally diverse neighborhoods of Queens. While the object of Gatsby's desire is Daisy Buchanan, and Kwang's is power, it is a major disappointment to each book's protagonist—Nick Carraway and Henry—when the object of their idolization is revealed to be corrupt. By shifting this classic tale to the modern setting of a New York borough and by adding complex themes of racial assimilation, Lee has taken a thoroughly American tale and made it his own.

As the novel's title suggests, language is of paramount importance in the novel. It is no coincidence that Henry's wife is a speech therapist. She is able to see through him, recognizing that he speaks with an overly attentive focus on enunciation. This reveals that he is not a native speaker; native speakers of language are freer and less studied in their pronunciation. Throughout, Leila stresses the importance of acquiring English as the best means of being integrated or assimilated into American culture. Further indicating the importance language plays in the novel, Henry's only mementoes of his son are the tapes that Leila has made with the equipment she uses as a speech therapist. When Henry takes over the role of Speech Monster at the end of the novel, he is actually confronting and working out his own uneasy relationship with language.

## Multicultural Settings

New York City and the outlying regions emerge as a character in the novel as well. Though Henry lives in downtown Manhattan, his father has made a home in Westchester (near the fictionalized town in which Gish Jen sets her novels, as symbolic of American affluence). Escaping New York means that one's assimilation into mainstream American culture is complete. Meanwhile, the complicated politics of New York's outer boroughs—mainly Queens—is a hotbed of confrontation as Italian, Hispanic, African, and Asian Americans fight for their interests and their right to be heard. When Henry leaves the relative safety of Manhattan for Queens, he is stepping into the heart of this diverse world, which provides both controversy in the novel as well as a backdrop to which Henry's experiences can be compared.

## *A Gesture Life*
### Summary and Analysis

From the first page of *A Gesture Life*, it is clear that the narrator, Doc Franklin Hata (or Jiro Kurohata, as he was known in his native Japan) will not be telling the complete truth. He says he lives just north of the city, in a town he will call Bedley Run, where he has resided for more than thirty years and where he believes he has become a highly respected figure in his small town.

Situations are described by the narrator that then do not correspond to his explanations of them. When Hata goes to visit the new owners of what used to be his medical-supply store, he is shocked to find himself unwanted, interrupting them, the Hickeys, in an argument. The store has been steadily losing money, and Mr. Hickey suspects that Doc Hata lied to him about the store's value. The new owner also accuses Hata of claiming to be a doctor. Doc Hata explains that he never said he was a doctor, that Doc is simply what the townspeople call him. Mrs. Hickey apologizes—the family is under pressure from the bank, and their son is in the hospital with a congenital heart defect waiting for a transplant. She asks about Sunny, the woman Hata's store was named after. Doc Hata replies that Sunny has gone back to Japan.

Hata lives in a valuable old Tudor house with a pool and well-tended gardens. Realtors frequently call him, including the pushy Liv Crawford. Returning from his outing, Doc Hata goes to Sunny's room, but he does not reveal the nature of his relationship with her. He decides to burn old papers, to purge the house of memories of her. He remembers the day he brought her home after adopting her, how she cried when she saw the old house, and how he fixed it up late at night after work so that it would be livable. He also recalls how he and Sunny never saw eye to eye, he forcing her to practice piano for her own good, she rebelling against his rigid control. As a teenager, she left home, finally estranging the two for good.

As Hata burns the papers and reminisces, Liv calls. He talks to her until he smells an odd scent. "The family room is on fire," he says calmly. Living nearby, Liv is able to arrive quickly and rescue him. The damage is not too extensive, and Hata, suffering from smoke inhalation, will be released from the hospital in a couple of days. He receives many visitors while there, including Renny Banerjee, the East Indian hospital purchasing manager, who reveals that he used to have a relationship with Liv. He also shares the bad news that a woman named Mary Burns has died and insinuates that she and Doc Hata used to be a couple. Hata feigns guarded surprise at the news but reveals to the reader that he was well aware she was ill, though he ultimately decided not to visit her in the hospital.

Hata explains how he and Mary met. She was a local widow, and they were both in their fifties. He revealed to her that he had no wife and had adopted Sunny from an orphanage. Mary became highly involved in Sunny's life but was always disappointed that Sunny remained distant and emotionally unresponsive. Hata was unable to explain that that had always been Sunny's demeanor, ever since she arrived in the United States. Mary was nonetheless able to diagnose the problem in Hata and Sunny's relationship: "It's as if she's a woman to whom you're beholden, which I can't understand. You're the one who wanted her. You adopted her. But you act almost guilty, as if she's someone you hurt once, or betrayed, and now you're obligated to do whatever she wishes, which is never good for anyone, much less a child." Mary hinted at a much darker psychology informing the relationship of Hata and his adopted daughter.

At the hospital, Hata enjoys speaking with candy striper Veronica, whose mother he knows. She is a police officer, whose new job is as a security guard at the local mall. She visits and mentions that she sees Sunny every day and that Sunny has a child, a fact Hata did not know. Hata then tells the reader a little more about the circumstances in which he was raised. He came from a poor Korean family and was raised by adoptive Japanese parents because he scored well enough on an exam to be eligible to go to Japan for schooling. After he came to the United States, he changed his name from Kurohata to Hata to save Americans the trouble with pronunciation. Though it was unconventional for a single man to adopt a female child, a bribe to the adoption agency helped him get custody of Sunny.

The police officer then reveals Sunny's misbehavior as a young woman, sneaking out at night and staying with Jimmy Gizzi, the local drug dealer. When Hata and Sunny got into a fight about the situation, she accused him of only caring about his reputation in the small town. "All I've ever seen is how carefully you are with everything. With our fancy big house and this store and all the customers. You make a whole life out of gestures and politeness." She revealed that she would not return home. Hata threatened to take away her allowance, to which Sunny responded, "I never needed you. I don't know why, but you needed me," a harsh echo of Mary's previous assessment of Hata and Sunny's relationship.

Sunny disappeared for three weeks, and Hata went to look for her at the Gizzi house. There was a party going on, and Hata wandered around, deafened by the music. The party began to take on the air of a dream, as Hata finally found Sunny, dancing in a suggestive manner for Gizzi and another man, seemingly part of a mutual seduction.

Hata then recalls an episode from the time he was stationed in Singapore during World War II. Following two friends to a brothel, he arrives to see an officer break the neck of one of the prostitutes. She is Korean, and hers is the first dead body he has ever seen. He helps the officer cover up the crime, and while he is waiting for his friends he sees a young woman running out of a room. She has a smear of blood on her thighs. He comforts her, speaking to her in the Korean he knows from his youth, telling her she has to go back into the room. She begs him for help, but he remains firm.

Liv arrives to pick up Hata from the hospital. Hata has arranged for Renny to join them, hoping to rekindle his friends' former romance. On the way out, he runs into Mrs. Hickey, who says they are giving the store back to the bank. Her son, Patrick, is in the hospital, and Mrs. Hickey begs Hata to visit him.

On the drive home, Liv and Renny discuss the racism present in the town, with Liv defending the people characterized as racist and Renny encouraging Hata to say that he, too, has experienced discrimination. Instead, Hata insists that he feels blessed by his welcome in the town, even though it took him a while to earn the community's trust. Liv has renovated his house, in an attempt to convince him to list the property with her real estate company, but Hata is not ready to sell.

Hata then remembers a time when Sunny came back to the house after a party. Her boyfriend Lincoln was accused of stabbing Jimmy Gizzi. She tells Hata she found a piece of black silk among his things, and he refuses to tell her its meaning. She hints that Gizzi raped her, which prompted Lincoln to stab him, but she will not elaborate or report it the police. Announcing her intention to move to New York City, she promptly leaves Hata's life.

Hata tells a story from the war, about a radio corporal by the name of Endo who is obsessed with pornographic photos. Hata humors him by looking at them but fears that the man has an unnatural obsession with the pictures. He also describes the others in the Burmese camp: Captain Ono, the doctor in charge, and Colonel Ishii. Everyone is excited because "Comfort Women" (prostitutes hired by the government to keep up morale in the camp) are arriving. Endo shows an inappropriate interest in the young Korean women, most likely virgins who are not the "volunteers" the army makes them out to be.

That evening, Endo and Hata are strolling, and they hear Captain Ono calling to a young woman who has hidden beneath his porch. She wants to be with her sister, she says, after being dragged out of her hiding spot. Ono grows increasingly impatient, prompting Endo to rush to her defense. Mistaken for a sniper, the captain's guard fires at Endo. Though he misses, soldiers, hearing the gunfire, arrive and shoot the captain's guard. A corporal joins them, leaning over the dead body with Hata. He asks Hata what he can do to prevent pregnancy, completely ignoring the hubbub around them.

The next day, Hata is supposed to examine the women for venereal disease. They are horribly bruised and swollen, and he cannot bring himself to touch them. He has little training as a medic and no familiarity with female anatomy. The young girl who was hiding the previous day keeps crying, and her sister, Kkutaeh (who had not spent the night with the commander, as she was not a virgin and therefore not as valuable), is raped on the examining table by Captain Ono. Outside, Endo is waiting and he rushes toward the women, grabbing Kkutaeh's sister and taking her to the outskirts of the camp where he slits her throat. The next day he is executed, given a sword to pierce his belly. When he does not commit suicide, the executioner cuts off his head.

The narrative then returns to the present. Hata is feeling depressed after his release from the hospital. Liv sends him meals every day, and he no longer swims or takes his daily walk. Renny comes for a visit and reveals that he and Liv have gotten back together, but her determination to marry him scares him. Among the pile of mail, one card is unsigned, presumably from Sunny.

Hata drives to the mall where Sunny works. He asks after her in the department store and learns that she will report for duty later. He decides it is a bad idea to visit her suddenly, but as he is leaving he has a coughing fit and waits on the bench to catch his breath. It is then that he sees Sunny, dropping off her son at day care.

She insists they go to the food court to talk; she is cold and distant. Hata learns her son's name: Thomas. They moved back to the area only six months ago. Sunny makes it clear that she does not want Thomas to know about Hata. She agrees that Hata can say hello, but he must pretend he is merely an acquaintance and not the boy's grandfather.

Here, Hata is possibly not telling the truth, both to the reader or to himself. He feigns that everything is fine but is actually listless and avoiding chores at home. He tells Sunny a story about a bank loan, and Sunny reminds him that Mary Burns's connections were the reason he got the loan, not his own reputation and hard work. What other things has he lied about? He and Sunny part with the agreement that he will call and come over to meet Thomas soon.

Hata babysits Thomas for an afternoon and spoils him at the toy store. Driving from the mall, the old man is reminded of the war again. Kkutaeh, known as K, was placed under Hata's care, to prepare her for the captain and a return to work at the comfort house. The other women are severely abused, but Hata is reprimanded when he tries to keep them in the infirmary and so he sends them back to the brothel. He is unable or unwilling to admit that his objections are moral and ethical or that he opposes the actions of the Imperial Army and his superiors. He is so divorced from his feelings that he refers to speaking to K in Korean as "speaking in her own language" when it is his native language too. "You are a Korean," she notes. Hata replies, "No, I am not. . . . I have lived in Japan since I was born," rejecting his heritage. He sees that K is an educated woman, from a more affluent background. She informs him that Captain Ono has not sent her to the comfort house. He touches her but not in a sexual manner. Hata finds this strange and an "egregious mark on the captain's *self-respect*, at least in the Japanese sense of the term." Captain Ono has increased his power within the camp, drugging the commander with painkillers.

K begs Hata to kill her before she is raped, but he tells her, "I am not your countryman. . . . And I will certainly do nothing of the kind." He recognizes he has romantic feelings for her. As the days pass, they grow closer, speaking of his childhood and hers and their dreams for the future. She tells how her father offered her and her sister to the army instead of her brother. They visit K's sister's grave.

The black flag appears, signaling that the captain will come for K that evening. She begs Hata to kill her or to run away with her. They can go to a foreign country, she suggests, like a couple in a western. Hata stiffens at the notion, though, reminding her that he is doing his duty. They lie down together, and while she pretends to sleep Hata begins to stroke her hair. She does not move or acknowledge him when he tells her he loves her. He assumes she is sleeping.

Hata then confronts Captain Ono about drugging the commander and sequestering K. The captain states that Hata knows nothing. When Hata says he will refuse to let Ono visit K, he responds, "You are an immense fool. I almost feel sorry for her." Ono explains that K has lied, that he has been sleeping with her and they have talked about meeting after the war. He tells Hata that K is pregnant, that she arrived pregnant, and her claim of virginity is a lie, just like everything else she has told Hata. Ono beats Hata for his insubordination. He takes out his pistol and holds it to Hata's head but does not pull the trigger.

Back in the present, Hata drives to Sunny's house to take care of Thomas while Sunny interviews for a new job. They begin to discuss the past, and the reason for their rift is made clear. Hata forced Sunny to have an abortion when she was 17.

Hata comes to realize that his means of dealing with the trials he has faced in life, his "well-planned response to life's uncertainties and complications," is a mere coping device and not a long-term solution. "After you have pushed aside and pushed aside and pushed aside again, the old beacons will bob up once more, dotting the waters before you like a glowing ring of fire." This statement proves true, as K appears as a ghost in his dreams, begging for his help.

In another flashback, Hata recovers from Ono's beating. He asks to see K's stomach, and she shows it to him, but she does not appear to be pregnant. Hata swears to protect her until death. When the captain arrives, K hints that Hata should shoot him or attack him with a scalpel. While Hata searches for the instrument, however, K produces her own scalpel and slits Ono's throat, killing him instantly. Again, she begs Hata to kill her. Taking a pistol, he shoots the dead Captain Ono instead. When the guards rush in, Hata says the captain shot himself accidentally. The guards drag K to the comfort house.

Unsure of how best to protect K, Hata goes to the comfort house to find her but is told everyone is at the clearing where Endo had killed K's sister. By the time Hata gets there, passing bloody soldiers returning from the clearing, there is little left of K's mutilated body. Hata begins to gather it for burial when he also finds a small fetus.

Back in the present, Hata has promised to teach Thomas to swim, and after a few lessons in the pool, they go to the beach where Thomas befriends other children. That morning, Hata received news from Renny that Mrs. Hickey was killed by a drunk driver while travelling home from a hospital visit with her son. Renny and Liv arrive. Hata notices that Thomas is swimming out too far, but Hata is distracted by Renny and Liv's announcement that they are getting married. They want his blessing, as the town elder. He recognizes, at that moment, how cut off he has become from his emotions: "I feel I have not really been living anywhere or anytime, not for the future and not in the past and not at all of-the-moment, but rather in the lonely dream of an oblivion, the nothing-of-nothing drift from one pulse beat to the next . . ."

A mother screams, unable to spot her son in the water, not knowing that he has gone to buy a hot dog. Hata realizes that he, too, cannot see Thomas. The adults rush in to the water to look for the boy. Hata sees that Renny is suffering a heart attack in the water but continues to search for Thomas, whose small body he finds unconscious in the deep water. Hata hands Thomas to lifeguards and then tows Renny back to shore. The lifeguards revive Thomas, and, although Liv is certain that Renny is dying, Hata is determined that no one will die that day.

Renny survives. Hata visits him in the hospital, avoiding Mrs. Hickey's son. He goes to her funeral, where Mr. Hickey fractures his leg. He sees Hata and says he will not let anyone touch him but "Doc Hata." Hata fears he is the cause of all this suffering. He believes that Sunny did the right thing, escaping from him years ago, and that he must now leave their lives or else "something terrible and final will befall them."

To his surprise, Sunny brings him sandwiches and tea. Though she is still angry, she has forgiven him, both for Thomas's accident and for his actions when she was a teenager. Hata drives home, remembering the teenaged Sunny's phone call begging for help to end her pregnancy. Instead of sending her money, he arranges for her to have an abortion after hours at the hospital. When she arrives, it is clear she is near her due date. Dr. Anastasia refuses to perform the operation, but Hata begs him, even offering to assist him. Finally the doctor relents, and Hata is forever haunted by the sight of the fetus's removal. Sunny leaves his house the next day.

Hata remembers the last time he saw Mary Burns. He perceived nothing wrong, but she, grown tired of his distance and detachment, leaves him with the words, "You're a marvel, I think." He decides to sell his house. He buys back the medical-supply store from the bank—relieving Mr. Hickey from its financial burden—as well as the apartments above, giving them to Sunny and Thomas to live in. He sets up a fund for the Hickey boy, an unlimited amount of money for his intensive care in the hospital. Then he plans to move far away, though it "won't be any kind of pilgrimage. I won't be seeking out my destiny or fate." Instead, he wants to "circle round and arrive again. Come almost home."

## Major Themes

### Storytelling and Truth

Chang-rae Lee's narrator is not to be trusted, making the notion of storytelling central to the novel. From the first page, he announces that he is inventing the name of the town in which he lives. While he would like to believe he is a respected and beloved member of the community, the town's residents may not view him with such reverence and high regard. He neglects to tell the reader important information, only gradually letting on that he adopted a daughter to atone for his guilt at not helping K during the war. He also withholds the fact that Sunny hates him because he subjected her to an illegal late-term abortion. The change he makes throughout the book, to view himself not with pride but with acceptance of his role in the harm he has caused, is the main realization the book presents.

Hata is unreliable, of course, because he is unable to face the truth and free himself from his burdening sense of shame. He is so removed from his own emotional life that he cannot recognize when others are suffering. It would be easy to suggest that this is in response to the tragedy he witnessed, but his cold, unfeeling nature is apparent even before the war, when he rejects his lower-class Korean origins and adopts the name and customs of the Japanese. He denies his nationality, even as he is speaking Korean to K, because he is ashamed.

## Emotional Detachment

Being cut off from or unresponsive to his feelings had once proved, to some extent, beneficial to Hata. It allows him to complete his duties as a medic in the war, even though the tasks he is expected to perform violate his personal sense of morality. He tells himself that he is a subordinate, doing his job, but in truth he is afraid to speak out. He lets K kill Ono, then allows her to be torn to pieces by the angry soldiers seeking revenge. "I felt a certain connection to her," he notes, "not in blood or culture or kind, but in that manner, I suppose that any young man might naturally feel for a young woman. This may sound ludicrous . . . under the circumstances, but I was youthful and naive enough that I possessed much more of a kind of hard focusing than any circumspection, which one may argue has remained with me for my whole life." Able to ignore the harsh realities and graphic violence to which he has been exposed (and failed to try and prevent), he relies on reason rather than instinct or feeling.

This lack of self-awareness is evident as he alienates Mary Burns. His relationship with her was a real chance to love and be loved in return, but he cannot offer her anything more than companionship. He continuously treats Sunny as a stern, disapproving parent would, always insisting that she improve herself and expressing no real feeling or sympathy for what she likes or wants. He cares for her in the sense that he provides basic comfort, but he is unable to love her unconditionally.

## Cultural Identity

In his novel, Lee brings up the idea of the "Asian character." Through Hata, Lee is able to explore the notion of racial stereotype. Hata is portrayed as obsessed with appearance, reputation, and defending his strong sense of pride. When he arrives in town, he worries that he does not fit into Bedley Run and is determined to carve out a place for himself, buying the nicest house and always greeting his fellow merchants.

> I wished only for myself that I could bear whatever burdens might fall to me, that I might remain steadfast in my duty and uphold my responsibilities and not waver under any circumstance, and by whatever measure. For I feared, simply enough, to be marked by a failure. . . . I have feared this throughout my life, from the day I was adopted by the family Kurohata to my induction into the Imperial Army to even the grand opening of Sunny Medical Supply, through the initial hours of which I as nearly paralyzed with the dread of dishonoring my fellow merchants.

He does not recognize that the townspeople have a duty to welcome him as well and make him feel comfortable. He feels instead that he must prove himself. He ignores the racial taunts and the obvious disdain people have for him, transforming it in his mind into a respect and an esteem he feels he deserves. His only real friend in the book, Renny, is a fellow immigrant, who tries to talk to him about the discrimination inherent in the town, but Hata refuses to admit he has been treated unfairly.

For Hata, assimilation means acceptance, the indication that he has finally found a home. Therefore, he changes his name to the more Americanized Franklin Hata and allows people to call him doctor, though he is not a medical professional. He is a Korean who tries to present himself, first, as Japanese, then as American, without knowing who he is as a person in the first place, apart from concerns of national or cultural origin. He tries to fit in in the army, though his morals conflict with those of the commanders and the organization overall. It is only at the end of the novel that he realizes how empty his life has been, that he has merely been going through the motions of living. Lee suggests, through his protagonist, that a life devoid of closeness, of feeling, is only the shadow of a life. "I think now that K wanted the same thing that I would yearn for all my days, which was her own place in the accepted order of things. . . . All I wished for was to be part (if but a millionth) of the massing, and that I pass through with something more than a life of gestures."

## The Abuse of Korean Women During World War II

A final but no less important theme is the novel's exploration of the horrible conditions faced by Korean comfort women during World War II. Forced to "volunteer," they were repeatedly raped and physically abused, treated as a form of supplies for the troops rather than as human beings. Though Hata believes there are similarities among all people of Asian descent, K sees only the violence, aggression, and abusive excesses of the Japanese soldiers. A shameful and underreported part of history, the story of the comfort women is finally revealed through this realistic and shocking portrayal.

# JHUMPA LAHIRI

## Biography

IT IS NOT often that a writer is given a major award for her first book, but that is exactly what Jhumpa Lahiri did, receiving the Pulitzer Prize for Fiction in 1999 for *Interpreter of Maladies* at the age of 32. Embraced by critics and readers alike, Lahiri may be the best known Indian-American writer working today.

Though she considers herself American, she was born in London on July 11, 1967. Her Bengali parents moved to the United States when she was three years old, and she grew up in Rhode Island where her father served as a librarian at the University of Rhode Island. She was raised in a home that emphasized Bengali heritage, while she was exposed to mainstream American culture at school. Like the protagonist Gogol in *The Namesake*, Lahiri used her "pet name" (nickname or commonly used name) instead of her "good name" (or official name) at school, because it was easier for Americans to pronounce.

Lahiri attended Barnard College and then spent several years accruing degrees from Boston University—M.A.s in creative writing, English, and comparative literature and a Ph.D. in Renaissance studies—all the while perfecting her craft as a fiction writer. In addition to the Pulitzer Prize, *Interpreter of Maladies* won the PEN/Hemingway Award and the O. Henry Award, among many others. Her second book, *The Namesake*, took on the story of the first generation of children born in the United States to an immigrant family. It was in many ways autobiographical. In it, the family splits their lives between two worlds, setting up residence in the United States while spending most holidays in Calcutta, which is where Lahiri's family is from.

In 2001, after stints teaching fiction at Boston University and the Rhode Island School of Design, she married Alberto Vourvoulias-Bush, who was then editor of *Time Latin America* and now serves as editor of *El Diario/La Prensa*. They live in

Brooklyn, New York, with their two young children, Octavio and Noor. In 2008, she published her second collection of short stories, *Unaccustomed Earth*, which debuted at the top of the *New York Times* bestseller list. In addition to writing, Lahiri also serves as vice president of the Pen American Center.

## *Interpreter of Maladies*
### Summary and Analysis

Critics of this collection of nine short stories praised the sharp, precise language and the perception and insight Lahiri brings to the characterization of her protagonists. Mostly of Asian descent, these individuals long for assimilation, standing just on the fringes of the New England world that has come to be their home.

The first story, "A Temporary Matter," deals with the breakup of a marriage. Shoba arrives home to find a notice that the power company is turning off the electricity for an hour that evening for repairs. Shukumar, her husband, has been home all day, supposedly writing his dissertation, but in reality spending most of the day in bed, obviously depressed. When Shoba remarks that they should cut power during the day instead, Shukumar takes it as a veiled insult.

For dinner, he is making a traditional Indian dish, but it will not be ready before the lights go out. Unlike their usual practice of taking their plates to separate areas of the apartment, they will have to eat together in candlelight. Shukumar worries they will have nothing to talk about. He notices that the pride Shoba once took in the house's organization has seemed to vanish.

Their relationship has been strained since their newborn died several months before. Shoba convinced Shukumar that he should go to a conference, the baby arrived early, by the time he arrived at the hospital, the child was dead. His mother-in-law's words, "You weren't even there," ring in his mind.

They eat, and Shoba suggests a game they used to play in India when she went to visit every summer. They each confess something they have never told the other. Shoba admits that when they were first dating, she looked in his address book to see if he had assigned her permanent space, which he had not. He admits that on one of their initial dates he forgot to tip the waiter and had to return the following evening, claiming he was distracted by the realization that he wanted to marry her.

The following evening, the electricity about to be cut off again, residents of the neighborhood sit on their porches in the last light of day. The couple does likewise. Over candlelight, they resume the game from the previous evening. Shukumar confesses that he once cheated on an exam. Shoba says she once escaped an evening with his parents by saying she had to work late; instead she went for a cocktail with a friend. The next evening, he confesses that he returned the sweater she bought him as a present and spent the money at a bar instead.

She says that once she let him talk to an important academic with food on his chin because she was angry with him.

The fourth evening reveals that when she was pregnant, he kept a picture of a woman cut out from a magazine. She admits she finds the one poem he has ever published sentimental. The game of confessions seems to bring them closer. The following night the electrical repairs are finished. They eat in silence with the candles lit and the lights off anyway. When dinner is over, she turns on the light and tells him she has found a new apartment and signed the lease. "He was relieved and yet he was sickened" that she had deliberately suggested the game in order to tell him so. He searches for a story that will wound her as deeply, telling her that when he arrived at the hospital, though she was sleeping, he held their baby and found out that it was a boy. He had promised himself that he would never tell her. They sit, at the conclusion of the story, at the table together, crying "for the things they now knew."

"Mr. Pirzada Came to Dine" is told from the point of view of 10-year-old Lilia. Her parents have a neighbor, the title character, over for dinner frequently. Though they speak the same language and eat the same foods, her parents explain that he is not Indian, but Pakistani, from Dacca. Her father cannot believe Lilia does not know about the division or the escalating tensions between the two countries.

Mr. Pirzada's wife and seven daughters have gone missing in the turmoil and migration. He is worried about them, and Lilia becomes concerned too. Every night, he gives her candy, which she eats in bed, letting the sugar stay on her teeth in order to cement her prayers for him. At school, she finds a book that mentions Indian history, but because it is not related to the topic of her report, her teacher tells her not to read it.

At Halloween, the family carves pumpkins. Lilia and her friend Dora trick or treat alone, causing Mr. Pirzada to express concern. When Lilia calls her mother from Dora's house when they are done, her mother is distracted. Lilia comes home to find Mr. Pirzada with his head in his hands. Civil war has broken out. Over the next few months, Mr. Pirzada no longer brings candy, and Lilia's mother makes simple dinners. They see less and less of Mr. Pirzada, and eventually he returns to Pakistan, later writing to Lilia's family saying that he has found his wife and children. Every night since his departure, Lilia has been eating candy in bed. Now, with the good news, her mother cooks a meal to celebrate his good fortune, and Lilia throws the rest of the candy away.

The title story, "Interpreter of Maladies," is third in the collection. Mr. and Mrs. Das have hired Mr. Kapasi to drive them and their children to the Sun Temple during their visit to India. Though they are of Indian origin, they are obviously fully American, dressing in shorts and T-shirts and carrying an English guidebook. Mr. Das explains that they have never been to India and are visiting their retired parents.

The car is not air conditioned, and Mrs. Das complains, hinting that Mr. Das is a cheapskate. Her annoyance increases every time Mr. Das asks to stop the car so he can take a picture. She files her nails and shoos away her daughter. In the car, she asks Mr. Kapasi if he is always a tour guide. He says that during the week, he interprets for a doctor who does not speak the local language, Gujarati. Mrs. Das says that his job has a romantic quality, the patients rely more on him than on the doctor. He says he has never thought of it in that way. Instead, he considers himself a failure because he has always wanted to interpret for diplomats and scholars. He began to interpret to pay off a bill for his son's illness. The son died, but the job stayed. Because his job reminds his wife of their dead child, she never asks about it. Mrs. Das catches Mr. Kapasi's eye in the rearview mirror, and he thinks they share a connection. Obviously, she and her husband are as unhappy as he and his wife are, remaining together for the children's sake. During lunch, Mrs. Das asks Mr. Kapasi to join the family. Mr. Das takes a picture of them, and Mrs. Das asks him to write down his address so she can send the pictures. She puts it in her purse. This thrills Mr. Kapasi, and he dreams of writing to her.

In an attempt to make the tour last longer, he suggests a trip to see local caves. He fantasizes about holding Mrs. Das's hand. When they arrive, Mrs. Das asks Mr. Kapasi to stay with her while the others explore the caves. She confides to him that her second son, Bobby, is not Mr. Das's child but the product of an affair with a visiting friend of his. She has never told anyone this secret. She asks him to call her Mina, because he probably has children her age. He realizes that she views him as a father figure and not a romantic interest at all.

He asks her if she feels pain or guilt over her infidelity, which offends her. She gets out of the car, unable to find Bobby when she reaches her family. Finally, Mr. Kapasi sees him. Monkeys are pulling at him, surrounding him and hitting him with a stick. Mr. Kapasi rescues him and returns him safely to his parents. When Mrs. Das takes out a brush to fix Bobby's hair, Mr. Kapasi's address flutters away.

"A Real Durwan" is the first story in the book to take place in India and feature solely Indian characters. Boori Ma sweeps and cleans the common areas of an apartment building in exchange for being allowed to sleep under the mailboxes. Each morning she drags herself up the four flights of stairs, complaining that her life was so much better before the Partition, the 1947 event that led to the declaration of India's independence from British rule and the creation of Pakistan. She describes the servants and fancy food she used to eat. Her loud laments wake up the residents of the apartment building, who gossip about Boori Ma. Some say she makes the entire story up. Others think that at one point she was a servant for a wealthy family she pretends to have been a member of. Still, they are happy to have someone who suggests "a real Durwan," a doorkeeper who lives on the premises. They allow her to come and visit, giving her food, but she is not allowed inside the apartments, as they do not want her fleas on the furniture.

One of the residents, Mr. Dalal, arrives with a surprise: two sinks. Because Mrs. Dalal says they have no room for two sinks in their small apartment, the second basin is installed downstairs. The next morning all the residents are lined up in front of the sink to brush their teeth. Soon enough, they grow resentful that the Dalals have a private sink while they are forced to share.

The Dalals go on vacation, with Mrs. Dalal promising to bring Boori Ma back a blanket. The wives embark on other improvements on the building. The workmen prevent Boori Ma from sweeping and tidying. She goes to the market, where she is robbed of her life savings. While she is gone, someone breaks in and steals the sink. The residents all blame her—why was not she around to watch the building? She tries to explain, but too many years of listening to her exaggerations make them doubt her. They decide now that the building is valuable, they need to get a real Durwan, and they throw Boori Ma out.

In "Sexy," Miranda and Laxmi are colleagues at a public radio station, where Laxmi is constantly on the phone. Ending her most recent conversation, she tells Miranda that her cousin's husband has just left her for a stranger he met while on a flight to London. Miranda had been on the phone as well, trying to decide where to meet her lover, Dev. The two first crossed paths at a cosmetics counter where he was buying makeup for his wife, who was leaving for India the next day on a long trip. They have seen each other every night since then, Dev being the first real adult male Miranda, at 22, has ever dated. During a visit to the Christian Science Center, they stand on opposite ends of a room in which an acoustical effect makes his whisper audible to her on the other side. "You're sexy," he says.

Miranda thinks of the only Indian family she knew growing up in Michigan. They were strange; she never played with the children. Once she was invited to a birthday party where the food smelled odd and she was terrified by a picture of the goddess Kali.

She buys lingerie she thinks a mistress would wear. Now that Dev's wife is back, he can only visit on Sunday afternoons. He barely notices her purchase. They eat, make love, and he departs shortly thereafter, leaving Miranda to think of him the rest of the week. She plans nothing for Saturday in anticipation of Sunday.

Miranda asks what Dev's wife looks like, and he mentions the name of an Indian movie star. She goes to an Indian store to look for her image. Meanwhile, Laxmi's cousin is distraught, her husband having demanded a divorce. Her cousin is going to California, and Laxmi convinces her to stop by Boston for a visit on her way. Laxmi makes reservations on Saturday for a spa visit and lunch at the Four Seasons. Miranda babysits her cousin's son. A demanding child who wants coffee, he then asks Miranda to quiz him on world capitals. He starts rummaging around her apartment, bored, and finds the silver dress she had bought to wear with Dev. He begs her to put it on, and she does, adding the stockings and high heels. The little boy tells her she looks sexy. She is shocked he employs the same word Dev had used to describe her. She asks him what that means. At first he will not tell her but finally relents: "loving someone you don't know." He says that is what his father did and the reason his mother is sad.

Miranda realizes the impact of her affair with Dev. As the child sleeps, she puts her jeans back on, crying. The following day, she tells Dev not to come over, saying she has a cold. She asks him if he remembers what he said to her at the Christian Science Center. "Let's go back to your place?" he guesses. Miranda is disappointed. The next weekend, a snowstorm prevents him from coming. The weekend after that, Miranda goes to the movies with Laxmi. Then, the following weekend she wanders around the city, ending up at the Christian Science Center, which is closed.

"Mrs. Sen's" features an 11-year-old protagonist named Eliot, whose mother is looking for someone to take care of him after school. Mrs. Sen advertises the fact that she is a professor's wife. She does not drive but will take care of Eliot at her house. Eliot's mother is not sure she feels comfortable with the fact that Mrs. Sen cannot drive, but her husband says he is giving her lessons.

Eliot is happy to go to Mrs. Sen's. Her house is warm in contrast to the frigid rooms in Eliot's beach house, which is lonely off-season. Also, Mrs. Sen is interesting. She tells him stories about her native India. She makes a sharp contrast to his mother who dresses in business suits. Mrs. Sen still wears saris.

Eliot watches in fascination as Mrs. Sen prepares dinner. When his mother comes to pick him up, she politely nibbles on a morsel Mrs. Sen offers but later confesses to her son that she does not like Indian food. Instead, she wants to eat the pizza she has ordered. The contrast between the home-cooked meal and the takeout pizza is obvious.

Eliot and Mrs. Sen settle into a routine. She picks him up at the bus stop. They practice driving around the parking lot, but never out into the busy street, and check the mail. Mrs. Sen loves to cook whole fish and misses the opportunity since coming to the United States. When she discovers a seafood market that will sell her whole fish, she asks Mr. Sen to drive her there. The next time she wants to go, Mr. Sen has office hours. Her tantrum summons him home, and he takes them to the fish store. He wants Mrs. Sen to practice driving, but she refuses because Eliot is in the car.

Mrs. Sen seems depressed. Her husband takes her and Eliot to the seashore, where the Sens buy so much fish that Eliot has to help carry them. They go to a restaurant and for a walk along the shore. On the way back, Mr. Sen insists that Mrs. Sen drive. She becomes flustered and confused and pulls over amid honking horns, refusing to drive any further.

When the fish store calls again, Mrs. Sen decides that she and Eliot will take the bus. On the way back, people complain about the smell, and the bus driver makes them open a window. Both are embarrassed. The following week, when the fish have arrived, Mrs. Sen decides to drive the two of them to the store herself. She starts by practicing driving around the parking lot. Then, to Eliot's surprise, she pulls out into traffic. She is nearly hit by an oncoming car, and in swerving to avoid it, she crashes into a telephone pole. Mr. Sen arrives to talk to the police, ignoring his wife. When they get home, Mrs. Sen goes to her room. Her husband returns Eliot's mother's check to her. She decides Eliot is old enough to stay at home by himself after school and gives him his own key.

"This Blessed House" centers on the arranged marriage of newlyweds Twinkle and Sanjeev. They are dissimilar in nearly every way. She is enthusiastic and outgoing, while he is pessimistic and introverted. Inspecting their new home, they find many religious artifacts, including figurines and paintings. Twinkle is delighted, while Sanjeev is offended; they are not Christian. She wants to keep a poster of Jesus with a crown of thorns. He demands she get rid of it—what will their housewarming guests think? She promises to hide it.

Sanjeev looks in the mirror, reminded that when she wears high heels, Twinkle is taller than he is. She claims she likes to wear high heels because she is at her desk all day working on her master's thesis. Sanjeev knows this is not true. He finds her reading in bed or sitting on the floor talking on the phone long distance during peak hours while a pot boils over on the stove. She is completely incapable of making traditional Indian food, feeding him precooked chicken and bottled salad dressing.

They clean up the yard in preparation for the housewarming party. Twinkle finds a statue of Jesus she insists on cleaning up and displaying outside. Sanjeev is worried that everyone will think they are Christian. He also wonders if he made a mistake in marrying Twinkle. Later, he decides to go into the bathroom while she is bathing and tells her he is taking the statue to the dump. She stands up in the bath and tells him she hates him and is going to leave him. She cries, and he apologizes. They agree to move the statue to the side of the house instead.

The party begins. As he feared, Sanjeev has to keep explaining that they are not Christian, despite the religious symbols in the house. He feels proud of the fact that his friends admire Twinkle's beauty. When Twinkle talks of treasure in the house, the guests want to go explore the attic. Angry, Sanjeev stays downstairs. Twinkle comes down carrying a huge silver bust of Jesus. She says she knows he will hate it, which he does, especially because it is obviously valuable. Still, he says nothing, carrying it over to the mantle as Twinkle wants.

"The Treatment of Bibi Haldar" again takes place in India, in a situation very similar to that of Boori Ma in "A Real Durwan." The story is narrated in the first-person plural—"we" or the voice of a group—creating the impression that the other residents of the apartment building are telling the story collectively. Bibi has been tortured all her life by seemingly incurable seizures and ill health. With both of her parents dead, she lives with her cousins, the Haldars. They treat her poorly, making her spend long hours in the rooftop storage shed taking inventory for their beauty shop.

Bibi constantly complains that she will never get married and is jealous of the other women in the building. They attempt to get her new clothes and makeup, but Bibi thinks such things are useless. After one particularly violent attack, a doctor says that in order to cure herself, Bibi must get married. The entire village laughs at the suggestion that only sexual relations will calm and cure her.

Bibi begins to prepare for her wedding, dieting and sewing clothing. Her cousins refuse to pay for her wedding picture, so the women in the building, doubtful she will find a husband, chip in. She places an advertisement, but no one responds. She is not particularly attractive, and her ailment is widely known.

When her cousin's wife gets pregnant, she fears that Bibi will curse the baby. After Bibi has another seizure, the wife forces Bibi to sleep in the storage shed on the roof. The women of the building boycott the cousin's beauty store in retaliation. When the newborn gets a fever, the cousins force Bibi to move back up to the roof again. Bibi claims to like the privacy and grows increasingly reclusive.

When the beauty shop fails, the cousins move out, leaving Bibi behind on the roof. The women in the building help her fix up the storage shed to be a bit more liveable but see little of her. They wonder if she is depressed, dying, or going insane. When one day they notice a trace of vomit, they find Bibi in her shed, pregnant. She gives birth to a baby boy, never revealing who the father is. There is much speculation but no evidence. She takes her cousin's inventory, sells it cheaply, and buys more, using it to support herself and her child. Above all, Bibi is finally cured of her condition.

"The Third and Final Continent" is the last story in the collection. The unnamed first-person narrator is an Indian immigrant telling his life story. After completing his education in London, at the age of 36, his parents decide, in 1969, it is time for him to marry. He is offered a job at the Massachusetts Institute of Technology. Now he has enough money to fly to Calcutta for his wedding and then to Boston. He stays at the YMCA in Boston in a miserable bare room. His wife, Mala, will arrive in six weeks, and he will have to find them a proper apartment. Intending to stay at the YMCA to save money until then, he sees an ad for a room in a house at a comparable price.

When he goes to see the room, the landlady, Mrs. Croft, proves to be an old woman who is going deaf and somewhat senile. She insists that he lock the door after coming in, saying it is imperative that he remember. She then notes, "There is an American flag on the moon!. . . . Isn't that splendid?" He decides to rent the temporary room, and when she tells him female visitors are not allowed, he announces for the first time, "I am a married man, Madam."

The narrator reveals details about his wife, Mala. She was old for a bride, 27, and though accomplished, "did not possess a fair complexion." Because her parents were worried she would never marry, they are willing to let her travel so far. For five nights after the wedding in Calcutta, the newlyweds shared a bed, Mala homesick and weeping. The narrator remembers his mother, whom he cared for as she died, slowly losing her mind.

Every day when the narrator returns home, Mrs. Croft asks him if he has checked the lock and makes him say that the moon landing is splendid. On Sunday, Mrs. Croft's daughter Helen comes to visit. Mrs. Croft demands that they come downstairs, as it is not proper for a woman and a man to be unchaperoned in a room. Helen laughs, saying she's sixty-eight years old. Mrs. Croft must be older than the narrator thinks.

Helen has brought her mother two bags of groceries. She opens several cans of soup and refills the two soup pots. Helen says that Mrs. Croft can no longer open the cans because her piano playing has given her arthritis. That was how she supported her family after Mr. Croft died. The narrator wonders how Mrs. Croft can only eat soup, but Helen answers that she gave up eating solids three years ago when she turned 100. The narrator is shocked to learn Mrs. Croft's true age and worries about her vulnerability. His own mother lost her mind when his father died.

The narrator keeps an eye on Mrs. Croft but can do little else. "I was not her son, and, apart from those eight dollars, I owed her nothing." Mala writes the narrator in preparation for her arrival, a letter in practiced English that does not affect him. He realizes he barely knows her and cannot even remember her face. Watching an Indian woman push her child in a stroller, the narrator witnesses a dog bite the end of her sari, unraveling it. He realizes he will have to teach his wife about life in the United States, reminding her not to let her sari drag. He worries that she will be homesick.

He gets an apartment appropriate for a married couple and moves out. Mrs. Croft gives him a simple goodbye. The narrator expected more but realizes that six weeks in the life of a centenarian means nothing. His wife arrives, and he gradually gets used to her presence. They settle into a routine. One evening, they walk to Mrs. Croft's house. Helen answers the door and asks if he will sit with Mrs. Croft who has broken her hip. She says she called the police, "What do you say to that, boy?" The narrator knows the answer, "Splendid!" he shouts, making Mala laugh. Mrs. Croft notices her. After looking her up and down she announces, "She is a perfect lady!" Mala and the narrator share a smile.

Time passes. When the narrator reads that Mrs. Croft has died, he is deeply affected and grief stricken. Mala and the narrator decide to stay in the United States and become citizens, their son eventually attending Harvard University. Driving to visit him, the narrator always takes Massachusetts Avenue so he can pass by Mrs. Croft's street. He remembers that there was a time before he loved Mala, when they were still strangers. At the story's conclusion, the narrator reminds his son that he has lived on three continents. He knows this is no great feat, but looking back on his life he is proud of his accomplishments and amazed that he has traveled so far.

## Major Themes

### Assimilation

The familiar theme of assimilation appears repeatedly in these stories, which all take as their protagonists people who have ties to India. Lahiri explores the various ways that immigrants and those born in this country become a part of or reject their society. There are those who seek to be integrated or fully immersed in their worlds, like Shukumar in the first story, "A Temporary Matter," going to the gym and eventually leaving her traditional, if loveless marriage. Sanjeev and Twinkle, in "This Blessed House," are able to enjoy and find humor in Christian religious icons. They realize they were not the first people or the first cultural tradition to have inhabited their home. In addition, Twinkle is an American woman who embraces her spirit and immodesty and stands up to her husband, which Sanjeev at times finds off-putting. Laxmi of "Sexy" is also a very Americanized figure, urging her cousin to leave her husband and planning the indulgence of a spa day. Mr. Kapasi of "Interpreter of Maladies" is surprised by how American the Das family seems, carrying a guidebook to India, distressed at a lack of air conditioning, and dressed immodestly in shorts.

At the other end of the spectrum are those who do not assimilate at all. Mrs. Sen spends all her time in the kitchen cooking meals that remind her of her homeland. She travels a great distance to get the whole fish she prizes and is completely reliant on her husband, hesitant and timid about learning how to drive. Her husband treats her like a child and is brusque and impatient with her. It is not a marriage of equals. In "Mr. Pirzada Came to Dine," the title character is representative of the temporary transplant—living in Boston, but only for a while, to study, using the United States as his college campus and dining only with other Indians. His real life is clearly not centered in the Western world.

Then, there are those characters who seek to balance and blend the various cultural influences they are exposed to. They negotiate the difficult space between maintaining their own heritage while fully participating in and entering American life. Shoba's husband, Shukumar, attempts to build a life marked by American and Indian influences, yet the couple seemingly reverses the traditional roles they grew up observing. Shukumar stays home and prepares the Indian dinner while his successful wife goes about her busy day. Finding himself in an unusual or unexpected role, he feels inferior and disconnected. Sanjeev has found success as a businessman but does not want to be seen as if he is betraying his heritage or trying too hard to fit in by following his wife's whim and installing Christian statuary on his lawn. He compromises in moving the piece to a less conspicuous place at the side of the house. The unnamed narrator of "The Third and Final Continent" gradually comes to enjoy his life in the United States, helped by the ancient landlady who accepts him unconditionally and reminds him of his mother.

The two stories that take place entirely in India and feature solely Indian characters—"A Real Durwan" and "The Treatment of Bibi Haldar"—engage the idea of assimilation as well. Both protagonists are outcasts and do not fit into their own society. Unmarried women have little power, so Boori Ma is unable to defend herself when she is blamed for the theft in "A Real Durwan." In her world, because she has no husband, she has no source of income or protection other than charity. She sleeps outside and is discarded when she is deemed no longer useful. Bibi Haldar also lives outside mainstream society because of her illness. She is unable to get married and so cannot participate in the life of the building. In an interesting and unexpected resolution, the cure for her illness is one that would not be condoned or approved of by Indian society. Unmarried, she gets pregnant and gives birth to a son. Yet this forbidden act is what finally cures her illness and allows her to attain a position in society. With a baby, she has respect and the newfound ability to support her family of two.

## Secrets and Confessions

An additional theme that runs throughout the collection is the guarding and revealing of secrets. In "A Temporary Matter," the two characters use the nightly blackouts as a safe space to confess what they have previously withheld from each other. At first, they reveal harmless secrets, but gradually the stakes are raised, and Shukumar tells her about holding their dead son, while Shoba confesses she is moving out. The secrets are revealed too late to save or preserve the marriage.

In the collection's title story, Mr. Kapasi takes Mrs. Das's confession as a sign of intimacy, but it actually serves the opposite purpose. She tells him precisely because he is outside her life, someone she will never see again and whom she views as inferior and inconsequential. When he is honest with her, telling her she feels guilty about cheating on her husband, he accurately interprets her "malady," causing her to storm off. The revelation draws her closer to her estranged family, even as it devastates Mr. Kapasi. In "Sexy," Miranda keeps her affair from her friend Laxmi because she knows Laxmi will not approve. Miranda even shields herself initially from recognizing the immorality of her actions. It is only when she sees the effect of infidelity that she is able to confront her own feelings of guilt and end the affair. Lilia, meanwhile, in "Mr. Pirzada Came to Dine," is embarrassed to be hiding candy; moreover, she is embarrassed to show so much emotion to Mr. Pirzada. Eliot, the protagonist of "Mrs Sen's," keeps his own secrets, not revealing to his mother that Mrs. Sen is behaving inappropriately or recklessly.

Secrets serve to drive the plots forward in many of the stories. Most secrets are kept to avoid hurting someone, but they fester over time. When they are finally revealed, the effect can be positive and cathartic, as with Mrs. Das's secret in "Interpreter of Maladies," or devastating, as with Shukumar's in "A Temporary Matter."

## The Compromises of Marriage

Most often in the collection, the secrets characters guard represent the alienation one spouse can feel from another, making the nature of marriage an equally important topic in the collection. Most of the marriages in Lahiri's stories are arranged. Sometimes the partners grow to love each other, like Mala and her husband in "The Third and Final Continent." Others seem destined to fail, like Shoba and Shukumar in "A Temporary Matter." Sanjeev's marriage to Twinkle in "This Blessed House" has an unknown future, surviving most likely only if Sanjeev can accept his wife's unconventional conduct and attitudes. Thoughout the nine stories, the strangeness of sharing a life with a virtual stranger, the awkwardness of creating a life from nothing serves as a source of conflict. Infidelity is a common occurrence in stories, usually stemming from loneliness or a lack of communication between partners. Lahiri provides her readers various glimpses of the difficulty faced in many modern marriages, using the Indian experience, in all its diversity, to search for universal truths about human love and interaction.

## The Changing Role of Indian Tradition

Indian traditions are also a central feature of the collection. Much of the characters' anxiety about assimilation stems from the clashes between two different cultures. The narrator in "The Third and Final Continent" has to take off his shoes inside Mrs. Croft's house, a custom that others find strange. The women's saris make them stand out as foreign and are inappropriate for the weather of the Boston area where many of the stories take place. American food and customs seem strange to the Bengalis, while the Americans fear or criticize the spices of Indian cooking. Creating meals reminiscent of home is a powerful way to keep the culture of India alive in Indian-American homes. For Mrs. Sen, the pursuit of authentic or traditional ingredients puts Eliot's and her own life in danger and leads to an accident.

The maladies of the title refer to an unhappiness in many of the characters that often goes undiagnosed. Mrs. Das, in the title story, seeks a remedy for her feelings of guilt, but she dislikes the diagnosis. The weight of secrets, of infidelity, guilt, loneliness, and unhappiness create, with varying degrees of success, a sense of uneasiness or a lack of emotional health that the protagonists seek to cure, with varying degrees of success, by establishing connections with others.

# The Namesake
## Summary and Analysis

*The Namesake* is Jhumpa Lahiri's second book and first novel. It follows Gogol Ganguli from his birth to Indian immigrant parents in Boston to his adulthood. Throughout, Gogol struggles with the expectations of his parents and his desire to fully embrace his American identity.

The novel opens in 1968 with a pregnant Ashima Ganguli making a traditional dish when her water breaks. At the hospital, she feels lonely and afraid. If she was still in Calcutta, her home until 18 months ago, she would be attended to by her entire family. Instead, in the United States, she goes into labor alone, without any relative on hand. She muses that Americans are so open but prefer to be alone when giving birth, one of the many overwhelming cultural differences she notes.

Ashima remembers the early days of her courtship with her husband. She returned home from school one day to be summoned to the living room where she could hear her mother praising her good qualities. She paused outside the door, noticing a pair of strange shoes that say "U.S.A." Intrigued, she put them on. She felt their heat and thought kindly of their unknown owner. Though her future husband averted his glance, as is proper, Ashima could sense Ashoke's curiosity. They were married two weeks later in a lavish ceremony and traveled to the United States, where Ashoke was studying.

While he waits in the hospital for his wife to give birth, Ashoke reads voraciously, remembering that his life was once saved by his bookworm habits. On a train, he met a man who drunkenly told Ashoke that he should travel the world. The man climbed into his bunk, as Ashoke continued to read "The Overcoat," a well-known story by Russian writer Nikolai Gogol. Then, in a horrific train crash, nearly everyone was killed. Rescuers saw the pages of the book flapping in the wind and tended to Ashoke. During his long recovery, he vowed to fulfill the man's suggestion.

The baby is a boy, and the Gangulis are surprised that they must name him before they leave the hospital. In Calcutta, naming ceremonies take place months after the child is born; some children are not named until they begin school. The honor of naming the boy goes to Ashima's grandmother; they await her letter revealing the name. Ashoke suggests Gogol as a pet name, in honor of his favorite author. His "good name" can wait. Ashima's culture does not allow her to disagree.

A visit from their landlords saddens Ashima. She does not want to raise the baby far from her family and friends, but Ashoke is firm. He will not let anyone dissuade him from traveling, and he likes the United States; India reminds him of his accident. Gradually, Ashima enjoys motherhood, finding a place in which she feels at home and reveling in her new independence. They are surrounded by many Indian friends.

At his rice ceremony, a traditional rite, Gogol does not pick any of the symbols that will predict his profession. He is indeed a product of the United States, free to choose his own destiny and invent his own identity. The letter containing his "good name" is lost in the mail and before it can be re-sent, Ashima's grandmother has a stroke and becomes senile. Gogol's official name, traditionally chosen, is lost forever. Ashima grieves to think that life is continuing in Calcutta without her.

When Gogol turns one, the family plans a trip to Calcutta, but before the travel date arrives, they receive a phone call informing them of Ashima's father's death. They must leave immediately, acquiring a passport for Gogol in his pet name instead of his good name. Ashima travels with trepidation; she is anxious to see her family and unprepared to witness their grief.

In 1971, Ashoke finishes his doctorate and is offered a professorship. The family buys a small house in a subdivision. Gogol is about to enter school, so Ashoke picks his good name. It would not be proper for him to be called by his pet name at school. He picks Nikhil—a traditional Bengali name that sounds like Nikolai.

Gogol, however, does not take to this renaming, and the school administrators revert to Gogol instead.

Gradually, though, Gogol becomes aware that his name is unusual and grows to dislike it. Why could he not be called by an American name, he wonders? When Ashima gives birth to a daughter, they name her Sonali, shortening it to Sonia, eliminating the problem. Gogol struggles with the "strange" Bengali customs his family retains. He suffers through Bengali classes and insists that his mother pack him traditional American lunches (bologna sandwiches) and make American dinners. When his class visits a cemetery to make rubbings on gravestones, Gogol picks the oddest names he can find, keeping the charcoal rubbings for many years.

Each year the family returns to Calcutta, a city the two children alternately find strange, foreign, and boring. They then return to the "modest house that is suddenly mammoth; . . . they feel as if they are the only Gangulis in the world." Still, their house "to a casual observer . . . appear[s] no different from their neighbors." Ashima and Ashoke's children also "sound just like Americans, expertly conversing in a language that still at times confounds them, in accents they are not accustomed to trust."

For Gogol's 14th birthday, in 1982, his parents throw him a party. He is disappointed. The party is full of his parents' Bengali friends—not his own. They make fun of a nerdy girl, Moushumi, who refuses to watch television with them, declaring in a British accent, "I detest American television." After the party, Gogol opens his gifts, disappointed at the pen sets and ugly sweaters. His father comes into his room with a special present, a valuable edition of Gogol's short stories. Though the boy knows his father admires the writer, he is disappointed to discover that Gogol is not even the author's first name. The boy thinks his name is totally absurd. The book is obviously important to Ashoke, who appears ready to tell him the story of the train accident but decides not to. Gogol puts the book on the shelf and promptly forgets about it.

Ashoke receives some good news: He has an eight-month sabbatical, which they will spend in Calcutta. Sonia and Gogol do not want to go—they have school, friends. Nonetheless, they find themselves on the plane, then sweating and bored at the various relatives' houses they stay at so as not to wear out their welcome. Ashoke takes the family to Agra to see the Taj Mahal, and the kids are delighted. In that region, all the Gangulis are foreign, and it is their first real vacation as a family. They have to hire a translator to explain the Hindi. Gogol, passionate about drawing, tries to sketch the dome.

After getting sick in Calcutta, like typical Americans, Sonia and Gogol are glad to get home and see their friends, none of whom asks about their trip. At school, Gogol encounters his first English teacher who knows about Nicolai Gogol, his namesake. He cringes in embarrassment when the story "The Overcoat" is assigned and does not read it. He is even more humiliated when he hears Gogol's life story: an eccentric genius unappreciated in his time, a depressed virgin who starved himself to death.

Gogol does not date anyone in high school, but when his parents leave him alone one weekend night, he goes to a college party. He assumes a new identity: he is "Nikhil" and goes to college. He meets a young woman who seems interested in his stories about India, and he kisses her, feeling like a person reborn.

About to start attending Yale University, Gogol changes his name officially to Nikhil and insists that his roommates call him that. The process is easy, and though he feels slightly guilty, he is relieved to be Nikhil, though the narrator continues to identify him as Gogol. On his way home one weekend, he meets Ruth, a fellow Yale student, on the train. They begin to date. He does not tell his parents about her, though, as he knows they will not approve of him distracting himself from his studies with a young woman, especially one who is not Bengali. He has already disappointed them by deciding not to major in engineering, taking art classes instead. Ruth studies abroad for a semester, but when she gets back, something has permanently changed in their relationship. They break up.

One weekend, Gogol goes home on the train and is delayed by a suicide on the tracks. He arrives two hours late to find his father waiting for him on the cold platform. In the car, Ashoke finally tells Gogol about the train accident that nearly killed him. Gogol is upset that his father never said anything. "Is that what you think of when you think of me?" he asks, as tears fill his eyes. "Not at all," his father replies. "You remind me of everything that follows."

In 1994, Gogol is living in New York City, pursuing a graduate degree in architecture at Columbia University. One night at a party he meets a beautiful blond woman. Maxine calls him the next morning, inviting him to dinner with her parents, Lydia and Gerald. Gogol cannot believe he is being pursued by a woman, and when he arrives at the house he is impressed by its size and its architecture. Maxine and her parents' home is different in every way from the Ganguli house. Maxine's house is in a state of lived-in messiness, filled with books from floor to ceiling and artifacts from trips abroad. Her parents are more like friends; together, the four of them finish three bottles of wine.

The two begin dating, and Nikhil practically lives at their house. "Quickly, simultaneously, he falls in love with Maxine, the house and Gerald and Lydia's manner of living." That summer, Gogol and Maxine plan to join her parents at their New Hampshire lake house. He has still not told his parents about living with Maxine, keeping his decrepit studio for appearance's sake. Ashima calls to let him know that Ashoke has won a prestigious appointment at a university in Ohio. Ashima surprises everyone by deciding to stay in the house outside Boston, alone. She will not have any friends or anything to do in Ohio. Maxine and Gogol stop for lunch on their way to New Hampshire. Gogol explains the rules—no touching or kissing in his house and no alcohol. The lunch goes well, though Gogol is uncomfortable. His mother asks him to call when they reach New Hampshire, but in the flurry of arriving and with the subsequent week of vacation activities, he forgets to check in.

By Christmas, Ashima has adjusted to her single life. She is alone but not too lonely, working at the library. Ashoke calls her. He is at the hospital, his stomach bothering him. Ashima does not worry, but when she does not hear from him, she calls the hospital. They inform her that Ashoke had a massive heart attack—he is dead. Ashima tries to call Gogol, but he is out for the evening. Finally, Sonia is able to reach him. She flies home from San Francisco to be with Ashima, while Gogol goes to Cleveland to identify the body.

Gogol moves in with his mother and surprises himself by adopting all the Bengali customs he had previous disdained. He dresses as a mourner and eats the special vegetarian diet. He pushes Maxine away and will not let her come to visit him. He ignores her requests to return to New York. He is wracked with guilt that he did not spend more time with his father when he was alive.

Maxine and Gogol break up after she is excluded from the ceremonial scattering of Ashoke's ashes in the Ganges River. Ashima insists that Gogol call Moushumi, the television hater from his 14th birthday party who has just moved back to New York. He stalls, busy with his architectural licensing exams, but finally succumbs to his mother's pressure. When they meet, he is amazed to find a mature, attractive woman. Moushumi has had bad luck with relationships as well. She was studying in Paris when she met her fiancé. But the pressures of a traditional Bengali wedding and other cultural differences proved too much for him.

With much in common, each the product of their overbearing Bengali parents, they agree to see each other again. Gogol is surprised by his attraction to her, impressed with her credentials as a scholar, and understanding of her need to push her parents away while simultaneously pleasing them. He buys her an extravagant present. She makes him dinner, a French recipe that burns when they go to bed instead of finishing the cooking.

They are married within a year in a traditional Bengali ceremony with a modern twist. With the money they amass from their wedding gifts, they are able to buy an apartment. Married life suits them, until they travel to France where Moushumi is to give a lecture. Gogol feels out of place and decides to spend time wandering around the city, having never been to Europe. He feels left out of Moushumi's life. This feeling of exclusion continues back in New York, where he finds her friends boring. During a discussion of names at a dinner party, Moushumi tells the story of the origins of Gogol's name, and he feels as though she has told his most intimate secret. He discovers, later, that Moushumi stayed with these friends after splitting up with her fiancé. He is not sure he really knows his wife.

Moushumi and Nikhil grow increasingly distant. She realizes she has been pushing him away, finishing her dissertation and teaching at NYU. Though she never tells Gogol, she has had to turn down a fellowship in France and feels resentful. Their first anniversary is a disappointment to her. Then one day she discovers the resume of an old friend, Dimitri, she had met when she was 17, on a bus to an apartheid protest in Washington, D.C. She had wanted to date him, but he seemed to want to be just friends. They remained in touch through the years via postcards and letters. The last she had heard from him he was living in Greece.

She calls him, they meet and start to have an affair. The guilt Moushumi feels soon fades. Gogol, meanwhile, still thinks of her all the time, unaware that she has been cheating on him and thinking of leaving him. On their way to Christmas dinner, Moushumi quotes Dimitri's views on Siena. "Who's Dimitri?" Gogol asks, figuring out by her reaction that the two are having an affair. "For the first time in his life, another man's name upset Gogol more than his own." Moushumi moves out.

Another year passes, and Gogol is traveling home for the last Christmas he will spend in the house in which he grew up. Ashima has decided to live half the year in Calcutta, the other half with her friends and children in the Northeast. Sonia is engaged. Gogol, in search of a camera, goes to his childhood bedroom, where he sees his father's gift, a copy of Gogol's short stories. He thinks that "in so many ways, his family's life feels like a string of accidents. . . . And yet these events have formed Gogol, shaped him, determined who he is." He feels his father's presence in the book, and, though Ashima tells him "this is no time for books," he opens it and begins to read.

## Major Themes

### The Search for Identity

*The Namesake* is primarily about the search for identity. The child of immigrants, Gogol is continuously negotiating the boundaries between remembering and honoring his Bengali heritage and embracing his American influences. It is the acceptance of both of these contradictory identities that finally provides him with the means of making his way in the world.

The most obvious example of identity in the book comes in the form of names. Because Gogol's official or "good" name is lost in the mail, he never receives a full Bengali naming rite. As a result, he is already stuck between two cultures. He is named after the book that saved his father's life, but his father only tells him this information when Gogol is an adult. When he changes his name, Gogol is assuming control of his own destiny. The fact that it is any easy switch to identify as Nikhil and that his parents put up little resistance indicates that, in truth, his identity has always been his own to figure out.

### Assimilation

Lahiri illustrates several different approaches to and representations of assimilation. At first, Ashima hates the United States. She finds both the weather and the people cold and the cultural practices confusing. She clings to Bengali ways, refusing to utter her husband's name and dressing in saris, impractical for the cold

Boston weather. Though Ashoke has the outside connection of work, Ashima is isolated in her American life and is unable initially to mentally leave the India she knows so well. She has only Bengali friends and continues to view life in the United States with a foreigner's eyes.

Meanwhile, the Gangulis have raised American children who enjoy watching television, listening to music through headphones, dating, and eating sugary cereal. Their first language is English, which will always be a foreign tongue to their parents. Also, like typical teenagers, they are embarrassed by their parents, feelings made all the more acute by the obvious differences their parents display or cannot hide: their accents, dress, and skin color. Gogol is also embarrassed by his mother's subservience and old-fashioned customs.

## Competing Cultural Influences

Gogol's parents understand that their children will be different. They have remained in the United States in part because of the educational opportunities available. Still, they are continuously disappointed by the lack of interest and respect their children show to Bengali culture. They maintain their original Indian-influenced expectations for their children, taking every vacation in Calcutta, forcing the children to be shuttled between and influenced by two worlds.

Gogol's name captures this mixture or blending of cultural influences. An Indian with a Russian name, he feels as if he stands out. When he discovers that Gogol is a last name of a depressed eccentric, his frustration and sense of being different increase all the more. It is only when he changes his name that he feels as though he is finally and truly himself, able to blend in.

Though his family is not fully American, the Gangulis do not entirely belong in India either. When Gogol and his sister go to Calcutta, they grow bored then sick in a society in which they do not fit in. Once again, they stand out, with their American clothes. The most cohesive time the family spends together is when they are in Agra. There, they are all foreigners, collectively out of their element and in need of an interpreter.

Gogol's two main relationships reflect this sense of being pulled by and stuck between two different cultures. Maxine is markedly different from the members of his family. Blond, American, with modern, sophisticated, wealthy parents who are permissive in a way Gogol cannot even imagine, he rejects his own parents in favor of hers. They understand and support his interest in architecture, while Gogol's own parents wish he had studied engineering.

In an important moment of change in the novel, when Gogol's father dies, he finds the Bengali rituals he had once resisted comforting. He returns home without being asked and observes the entire mourning period. Suddenly, he sees the value of his heritage and realizes what an important and defining part of his life it is. As a result of this growth and realization, he breaks up with Maxine and does not want her to come to Calcutta to spread his father's ashes. He decides she is not part of his family, even though she has welcomed him into hers.

In embracing his Indian side, Gogol moves into a new sphere of influence and identity. Moushumi is just like him, an educated American struggling with the restrictions placed on her by her Indian parents. She is sophisticated and intellectual and shares the same out-of-focus sense of identity that he does. By marrying her in a traditional ceremony, they both affirm their heritage. The marriage, however, is not destined to last. Too much alike, each finds in the other the same disappointments that have always plagued their search for a stable, embraceable identity.

## The Importance of Family

At the heart of the novel's exploration of culture and identity lies the family. Gogol's family exerts a strong pull, one that he must actively work against in order to unearth his true nature and identity. This familial influence is so strong that Gogol must change his name to escape it. He chooses Maxine in part because she stands in stark contrast to his family; by being with her he is symbolically rejecting the Gangulis and their heritage. He sees, however, that his choice of a love interest is too radical and that she could never really be a part of his family. Though he feels at home in her world, his will always remain a cultural experiment to her. He seeks out Moushumi to fulfill his parents' expectations that he will marry a Bengali woman, but that experiment fails as well. It is only when he no longer makes decisions to spite or please his parents that he is able to be at peace with himself.

Lahiri presents life as a series of accidents, or coincidences. Gogol often thinks that his life would have been different had his mother not been fascinated by his father's shoes, if his father had not been reading Gogol on the train, if the accident had taken his life. Though not superstitious, Gogol sees how accidents shape and deeply influence the future. Eventually, at the end of the novel, he returns to the past, rebuilding his life by reading the collection of short stories that helped lay the initial groundwork for who he is.

# CHRONOLOGY

## 1830s
- The first Chinese immigrants living in the United States include sugar workers in Hawaii and sailors and peddlers in New York.

## 1844
- First treaty established between the United States and China.

## 1848
- The gold rush in California attracts Chinese miners.

## 1854
- Yung Wing graduates from Yale University. He is the first Chinese graduate of an American college.
- The United States and Japan sign their first treaty.

## 1858
- A California anti-immigration law prohibits the entry of Chinese and "Mongolians."

## 1865
- The Central Pacific Railroad Company brings Chinese workers to the West to construct the transcontinental railroad.

## 1868
- The Burlingame-Seward Treaty between the United States and China allows citizens to emigrate.

## 1877

- Anti-Chinese violence erupts in Chico, California.

## 1878–80

- A series of laws known as "Chinese exclusion laws" is passed, intended to deny Chinese citizens rights of citizenship and immigration.

## 1882

- The United States announces no immigrant laborers will be admitted to the country for ten years.
- The United States and Korea sign their first treaty.

## 1885

- Anti-Chinese violence in Rock Springs, Wyoming Territory, results in many Chinese deaths.

## 1886

- Many western towns expel their Chinese residents.

## 1892

- The Geary Law extends the exclusion of Chinese laborers for another ten years and requires all Chinese to register.

## 1898

- The court case *Wong Kim Ark v. the United States* rules that American-born Chinese cannot be stripped of their citizenship.
- The Spanish-American War ends with the Philippine Islands becoming a protectorate of the United States.
- Hawaii is annexed by the United States.

## 1900

- Japanese plantation workers in Hawaii begin migrating to the mainland.

## 1903

- The first group of Korean workers, approximately 7,000 in total, arrives in Hawaii to work as strikebreakers and replace Japanese laborers.

## 1906

- A devastating earthquake in San Francisco destroys all birth and immigration records. Chinese men register as citizens and many of their wives and children leave China to join them.

## 1907
- Japan and the United States reach an agreement: Japan will no longer issue passports to Japanese wishing to immigrate to the United States.

## 1910
- The first restrictions on Asian Indians entering California are put into effect.

## 1917
- Immigration law declares Asia a "barred zone" and no immigrant from the continent is allowed to enter the country.

## 1918
- Asian veterans of World War I are allowed to naturalize.

## 1922
- Laws are passed revoking citizenship to those who marry Asian aliens.
- High courts uphold alien land acts that bar immigration and naturalization.

## 1923
- John Okada is born in Seattle.

## 1924
- The Immigration Act denies entry to virtually all people of Asian descent.

## 1934
- Starting this year, a maximum of 50 Filipino immigrants are allowed to enter the country annually.

## 1940
- Maxine Hong Kingston and Bharati Mukherjee are born.

## 1941
- On December 7, Japanese planes attack Pearl Harbor, Hawaii. The United States enters World War II.
- 2,000 Japanese community leaders are rounded up and interned in camps. By the end of the war, more than 110,000 Japanese Americans will be interned.

## 1943
- Chinese exclusion laws are repealed by the U.S. Congress. Chinese immigrants are granted the right to naturalize. The limited immigration quota remains at 105 people per year.

## 1944
- Americans of Japanese descent are drafted.

# 1945

- On August 6, the United States drops the atomic bomb on Hiroshima, Japan, marking the first use of a nuclear weapon.
- On August 9, Nagasaki is bombed.
- On August 14, World War II ends in the Pacific theater with Japan's surrender.

# 1946

- A limited number of Asian Indians and Filipinos are granted the right to immigrate and naturalize.
- In Arizona, Wing F. Ong becomes first Asian American to be elected to state office.
- The Philippines becomes independent; all Filipinos living in United States become eligible for citizenship.

# 1947

- The amendment to the 1945 War Brides Act allows Chinese-American veterans to bring foreign wives into the United States.

# 1949

- Diplomatic ties between the United States and China break down after Communists gain control and form the People's Republic of China.
- Five thousand mostly highly educated Chinese living in the United States are granted refugee status.

# 1950–53

- The Korean War results in the peninsula being divided into two seperate nations.

# 1952

- Amy Tan is born.

# 1956

- Gish Jen is born on Long Island, New York.
- Ha Jin is born February 21 in China.

# 1957

- John Okada publishes *No-No Boy.*

# 1965

- Immigration law declares it illegal to consider "national origins" in immigration quotas.
- Chang-rae Lee is born.

# 1967

- Jhumpa Lahiri is born July 11, as Nilanjana Sudeshna Lahiri, in London.

## 1961

- The U.S. military arrives in Vietnam; some consider this the beginning of the Vietnam War.

## 1968–69

- Students strike in California to demand the establishment of ethnic studies programs, including those devoted to Asian Americans.

## 1971

- John Okada dies.

## 1975

- The United States receives more than 130,000 refugees from Vietnam, Kampuchea (present-day Cambodia), and Laos as the Vietnam War ends.

## 1976

- Maxine Hong Kingston publishes *The Woman Warrior: Memoirs of a Girlhood among Ghosts*, which wins a National Book Critics Circle Award.

## 1979

- The People's Republic of China and the United States establish diplomatic ties.

## 1980

- Due to the overwhelming number of refugees from Vietnam and Laos, the United Nations helps organize immigration.
- Maxine Hong Kingston publishes *China Men*, which wins the 1981 National Book Award for general nonfiction.

## 1981

- The Commission on Wartime Relocation and Internment of Civilians declares the internment of Japanese Americans a "grave injustice" motivated by "race prejudice, war hysteria and a failure of political leadership."

## 1987

- The U.S. House of Representatives makes an official apology to Japanese Americans who were interned. Each surviving internee receives $20,000 in reparations.

## 1988

- Bharati Mukherjee publishes *The Middleman and Other Stories*, which wins the National Book Critics Circle Award for fiction.

## 1989

- The United States reaches an agreement with Vietnam that allows political prisoners to immigrate.

- The Tiananmen Square uprising in China leads to many civilian deaths.
- Bharati Mukherjee publishes *Jasmine*.
- Maxine Hong Kingston publishes *Tripmaster Monkey: His Fake Book*.
- Amy Tan publishes *The Joy Luck Club,* which is later made into a motion picture.

## 1990
- Ha Jin publishes *Between Silences*, a book of poems.

## 1991
- Gish Jen publishes *Typical American*.
- Amy Tan publishes *The Kitchen God's Wife*.

## 1995
- *Native Speaker* is published by Chang-rae Lee.
- Amy Tan publishes *A Hundred Secret Senses*.

## 1996
- Gish Jen publishes *Mona in the Promised Land*.
- Ha Jin publishes *Facing Shadows,* his second book of poetry, and *Ocean of Words,* a novel, which wins the PEN/Hemingway Award.

## 1997
- Ha Jin publishes *Under the Red Flag*, a book of stories.

## 1999
- Chang-rae Lee publishes *A Gesture Life*.
- *Gish Jen* publishes *Who's Irish?: Stories*.
- Ha Jin publishes *Waiting,* which wins the National Book Award and the PEN/Faulkner Award.
- Jhumpa Lahiri publishes *Interpreter of Maladies*, which wins the Pulitzer Prize for Fiction. She is the first person of Asian descent to win the award.

## 2001
- Ha Jin publishes *Wreckage*, a book of poems.
- Amy Tan publishes *The Bonesetter's Daughter*.

## 2002
- Bharati Mukherjee publishes *Desirable Daughters*.

## 2003
- Maxine Hong Kingston publishes *The Fifth Book of Peace*.
- Jhumpa Lahiri publishes *The Namesake*.

## 2004
- Chang-rae Lee publishes *Aloft*.
- Ha Jin publishes *War Trash*.

## 2005
- Amy Tan publishes *Saving Fish from Drowning*.

## 2008
- Ha Jin publishes his first book of essays, *The Writer as Migrant*.
- Jhumpa Lahiri publishes *Unaccustomed Earth*, a collection of stories.

## 2009
- Ha Jin's *A Good Fall: Stories* is published.

## 2010
- Chang-rae Lee publishes *The Surrendered*.

## *America Is in the Heart* by Carlos Bulosan

Though this author is primarily a poet, his semiautobiographical novel is known for its portrayal of a Fillipino protagonist who comes to the United States to work as a migrant laborer in the years before World War II. The main character is confronted by racism as he tries to find his place in the rural West.

## *American Woman* by Susan Choi

In this thinly veiled account of the Patty Hearst kidnapping in 1974, Jenny Shimada is a Japanese-American woman guilty of bombing a draft office, who is put in charge of housing Patty (here called "Pauline") and her captors. As Jenny reconsiders her role as a radical, she engages in a uniquely American attempt to reinvent herself, even as she trains to overthrow the system.

## *The Barbarians Are Coming* by David Wong Louie

Sterling Lung is a French-trained chef whose immigrant parents are disappointed that he did not become a doctor. They, as well as society, encourage him to be more Chinese, though he feels fully American. When his girlfriend becomes pregnant, Sterling has to decide what kind of a parent, and son, he wants to be.

## *Book of Salt* by Monique Truong

Bonh is a Vietnamese chef who answers an ad placed by Gertrude Stein and Alice B. Toklas in this historically based novel. In Truong's interpretation, Bonh is a homosexual, exiled from his homeland and saddened by his past. His sensual recipes form a backdrop to his memories, as the overwhelming loss of his home country continues to plague him.

## *And China Has Hands* by H.T. Tsiang

Wong Wan-Lee arrives in the United States in the 1930s in search of work, love, and a home, three difficult tasks in a country crippled by depression, citizens afraid and prejudiced against Chinese workers, and a mostly male population. He flits from one adventure to the next, while Tsiang creates a lively portrait of Chinese immigrant life before World War II.

## *Cebu* by Peter Bacho

Priest Ben Lucero takes his mother's remains back to her homeland in the Phillipines for burial. There, he is introduced to the differences in his American version of Filipino culture and the culture as it actually exists on the island. He is shocked at the violence plaguing the nation and returns to the United States to find similar unrest at home, making him feel as though he is at home in neither society.

## *Edinburgh* by Alexander Chee

This emerging author's first novel tells the story of a Korean-American boy molested by his choir teacher. He must come to terms with his troubled past when he meets the teenaged son of his molester and confronts the lasting effects of the abuse and his true sexuality.

## *Facts for Visitors* by Srikanth Reddy

This book of poetry discusses the idea of the present, in its myriad forms. Born in the United States and of Indian descent, Reddy investigates a global identity. Part political commentary, part keen observation, the poems frequently use traditional forms to comment on a new and changing world.

## *FOB* by David Henry Hwang

This play highlights the differences between fully assimilated Asian Americans and recent immigrants (deemed fresh off the boat). It won an Obie Award in 1980 for its complicated portrayal of the immigrant experience and its innovative mix of traditional Chinese mythology and modern theatrical techniques.

## *Golden Mountain Chronicles* by Laurence Yep

Yep is a young adult novelist whose most famous series of books follows the Young family during its travels from China in the 19th century to the middle of the 20th century. Yep's use of science fiction, fantasy, and history earned him a Newbery Award.

## *Hunger* by Lan by Samantha Chang

This novella and stories take as their subjects the Chinese-American immigrant experience but also the relationship among the various generations. While the immigrant generation attempts to erase the past and hide its hurts, its offspring are interested in figuring out where they came from in order to understand who they are.

## *Madeline Is Sleeping* by Sarah Shun-Lien Bynum

This experimental novel was a finalist for the National Book Award. Told in a mix of prose poems, dreams, and narrative, the title character overcomes a disfigurement caused by her mother, only to join a circus in rural France. Throughout, she struggles to be neither victim nor victimizer and, in doing so, finds her own true self.

## *M. Butterfly* by David Henry Hwang

Drawing on a true story, this popular award-winning play is the story of a French diplomat who carried on an affair with a Chinese opera singer for 20 years, believing her to be a woman. In 1986, he was charged with treason when his lover was revealed to be a male spy. Hwang references and transforms the story of the opera *Madame Butterfly* to examine Western notions of Eastern beauty and culture.

## *The Phoenix Gone, the Terrace Empty* by Marilyn Chin

Chin's poetry traces the complicated connections between East and West, feminine and masculine. Her work is often overtly political and deals with postcolonial attitudes toward assimilation and integration.

## *The Samurai's Garden* by Gail Tsukiyama

Twenty-year-old Stephen arrives in a small village in Japan to recuperate from tuberculosis. As tensions between Japan and China escalate, he forges friendships with the islanders, who include a gardener, a leper, and a young woman. Stephen questions the notions of duty, nationality, honor, and loyalty as the rural village gets caught up in much larger historical events.

## *Sightseeing* by Rattawut Lapcharoensap

These seven coming-of-age stories are all set in Thailand as their young male protagonists negotiate a world of beauty and poverty, duty, and desire.

## *Stealing Buddha's Dinner* by Bich Minh Nguyen

This memoir recounts the childhood of its author, who emigrated from Vietnam when she was 8 months old. Her father, having remarried after leaving his first wife in

Vietnam, is a distant figure, and Bich negotiates the worlds between Vietnam and the United States, between father and stepmother, and between Vietnamese and American cuisine.

## *Stories of Your Life and Others* by Ted Chiang

This debut collection of stories by Chiang, an author of Chinese descent, takes its place firmly in the genre of speculative fiction. In each, an aspect of history or science leads to a reimagined world, where right and wrong are more difficult to identify than they seem.

## *Summer of the Big Bachi* by Naomi Hirahara

Japanese-American gardener Mas Arai is the protagonist of this mystery novel set in Pasadena, California. Catapulted into a search for other survivors of the atomic bomb in Hiroshima, Arai wonders if *bachi*, karmic retribution, is at work in his life.

## *A Thousand Years of Good Prayers* by Yiyun Li

These stories are set in many different locations, from China to Chicago, as their protagonists explore the complications of marriage, immigration, and the legacy of the Cultural Revolution. Told in a sparse style by an author who learned English as a second language, these tales reveal the inherent cultural differences we all experience.

## *Tripmaster Monkey, His Fake Book* by Maxine Hong Kingston

This is the story of Wittman Ah Sing, whose drug-fueled travels through 1960s San Francisco provide fodder for a wildly inventive novel. In the space of a few days, Wittman gets fired from his job, marries to avoid the draft, and stages an improvisational play based on Chinese myth, ending with a monologue about what it is to be Chinese American.

## *Typical American* by Gish Jen

This novel relates Ralph Chang's journey to the United States and the compromises he makes in the search for assimilation. In losing his "Chinese way," he loses his sense of self, which threatens to destroy the typically American life he inhabits.

# BIBLIOGRAPHY

## Critical Sources

Cheung, King-Kok. *Articulate Silences: Hisaye Yamamoto, Maxine Hong Kingston, Joy Kogawa*. Ithaca, NY: Cornell University Press, 1993.

———. *An Interethnic Companion to Asian American Literature*. New York: Cambridge University Press, 1997.

Grice, Helena. *Negotiating Identities: An Introduction to Asian American Women's Writing*. Manchester, England: Manchester University Press, 2002.

Ishizuka, Kathy. *Asian American Authors*. Berkeley Heights, NJ: Enslow Publishers, 2000.

Lowe, Lisa. *Immigrant Acts: On Asian American Cultural Politics*. Durham, NC: Duke University Press, 1996.

Ma, Sheng-Mei. *The Deathly Embrace: Orientalism and Asian American Identity*. Minneapolis, MN: University of Minnesota Press, 2000.

Nelson, Emmanuel S., ed. *Asian American Novelists: A Bio-Bibliographical Critical Sourcebook*. Westport, CT: Greenwood Press, 2000.

Said, Edward. *Orientalism*. New York: Vintage, 1979.

Solano Munoz, Romeo. *Filipino Americans: From Invisibility to Empowerment*. Chicago: Nyala Publishing, 1996.

Tan, Amy. "Best-selling writer Amy Tan reflects on childhood memories." Interview with Kerry O'Brien. *7:30 Report*. Australian Broadcasting Corporation. 17 May, 2001. TV Program transcript. <http://www.abc.net.au/7.30/content/2001/s298666.htm>

Wong, Sau-Ling Cynthia. *Reading Asian American Literature: From Necessity to Extravagance*. Princeton, New Jersey: Princeton University Press, 1993.

## Anthologies

Chan, Jeffrey Paul, Frank Chin, Lawson Fusao Inada, and Shawn Wong, eds. *The Big Aiiieeeee!: An Anthology of Asian American Writers.* New York: Penguin, 1995.
Hongo, Garrett, ed. *The Open Boat: Poems from Asian America.* New York: Anchor Press, 1993.

## Web Sites

Asian American Literature: Resources for Research
http://www.sjsu.edu/faculty/awilliams/AsianAmResources.html

Chinese-American Literature Information Resources Guide
http://library.uhh.hawaii.edu/research_tools/guides/chi_amer_literature.htm

The History of Japanese Immigration
http://brownvboard.org/brwnqurt/03–4/03–4a.htm

In Search of *No-No Boy*
http://www.resisters.com/nonoboy/teachers/classroom_guide.pdf

Japan's Modern History: An Outline of the Period
http://afe.easia.columbia.edu/japan/japanworkbook/modernhist/outline.html

John Okada: Finding Identity in Betrayal
http://www.goldsea.com/Personalities/Pigs/okadaj.html

Minority Literatures
http://vos.ucsb.edu/browse.asp?id=2746#id286

# INDEX

# PICTURE CREDITS

# ABOUT THE AUTHOR

A Chicago native, **ALLISON AMEND** majored in comparative literature (Latin American and French literature) at Stanford University. She received an M.F.A. from the University of Iowa Writers' Workshop. Her fiction has received awards from and appeared in *One Story, Black Warrior Review, StoryQuarterly, Bellevue Literary Review, The Atlantic, Prairie Schooner,* and *Other Voices,* among other publications. She is the author of *Things That Pass for Love* (OV Books, 2008) and *Stations West* (LSU Press, 2010). Visit her on the Web at www.allisonamend.com